Trial of John J

Lay precentor of Cloisterham

Cathedral in the County of Kent

For the murder of Edwin Drood, engineer

G. K. Chesterton

J. W. T. Ley

Alpha Editions

This edition published in 2024

ISBN : 9789362095855

Design and Setting By
Alpha Editions
www.alphaedis.com
Email - info@alphaedis.com

Contents

INDICTMENT OF JOHN JASPER

Lay Precentor of Cloisterham Cathedral, in the County of Kent,

for the

MURDER

of

EDWIN DROOD, *Engineer.*

TRIAL

Holden at the ASSIZES at WESTMINSTER,
on the 7th January, 1914.

ASSIZE COURT	}	To wit:
KING'S HALL, COVENT GARDEN		
County of LONDON		

The Jurors for this trial upon their oath[1] present, that JOHN JASPER on the 24th day of December in the year of our Lord One thousand eight hundred and sixty in the Parish of Cloisterham and within the jurisdiction of the said Court, feloniously, wilfully, and of his malice aforethought did kill and murder one EDWIN DROOD against the peace of every true Dickensian.

FOOTNOTES:

[1] Or, if one of the Grand Jurors be a Quaker or other person entitled to affirm instead of taking an oath, say instead: "The jurors of Our Lord the King upon their oath *and affirmation* present, &c."

INDICTMENT

WHEREAS, in support of the above Indictment, divers allegations are set forth, as follows, that is to say:—

The accused, JOHN JASPER, aged 26, is Choirmaster at Cloisterham Cathedral, otherwise known as "lay precentor." He lodges over the Gateway of the Cathedral. For some years he admits he has been in the habit of taking opium, and has resorted to an Opium Den in the East End of London kept by an elderly woman known as "Princess Puffer."

The man of whose murder he stands accused was his nephew, EDWIN DROOD, in his 21st year, and by profession an Engineer. The Prisoner, who was likewise Trustee and Guardian of the said Edwin Drood, professed the greatest affection for him, and on the occasion of his visits to Cloisterham manifested every appearance of joy and satisfaction.

The said Edwin Drood was betrothed to one Rosa Bud, this being in fulfillment of a contract made by their respective parents (now deceased). Certain formalities in connection with the confirmation of this engagement, notably the handing of a ring by Mr. Grewgious, solicitor, Staple Inn, legal adviser to Edwin Drood, were witnessed by Mr. Grewgious's clerk, Bazzard. There is evidence to show that they had grown weary of each other, and wished the Contract to be annulled. On the other hand, Jasper, the Accused, was admittedly in love with Rosa Bud, and it is alleged was secretly jealous of his nephew. Miss Bud, on her part, deposes that she not only disliked but "feared" Jasper and avoided his attentions as much as possible. Eventually the engagement between Edwin Drood and Rosa Bud was rescinded by mutual consent; but the said John Jasper, for sufficient reasons, was not at the time warned of this fact. The circumstance, however, was revealed to Mr. Grewgious.

WITNESSES will be called to prove that in the early part of the year, the Accused, Jasper, accompanied a stonemason named Durdles to the Cathedral and made particular enquiry into the destructive qualities of quicklime. It is also alleged that Jasper applied a drug to this same Durdles, causing sleep, and that he then appropriated his keys, and therefrom made a close investigation of the vaults, especially of the Sapsea vault, which was partly hollow.

There were also residing in Cloisterham an orphan brother and sister, twins, by name Neville and Helena Landless. They came from Ceylon, where they had been subjected to personal ill-treatment, and after staying with Mr. Honeythunder, their guardian, Neville was lodged with Canon Crisparkle, and Helena was sent to Miss Twinkleton's school. Neville Landless is described as "fierce" and hot-blooded, Helena Landless is "almost of the gipsy type." Between her and her brother is a strong bond of affection. In her girlhood she had escaped at times from her cruel step-father by disguising herself as a boy. She is a woman of much daring.

Soon after their arrival in Cloisterham, they met Drood, Jasper and Miss Bud at a party. It will be given in evidence that there was a contention between Drood and Neville, and that Jasper afterwards fomented the ill-feeling and charged Neville Landless with being "murderous." At the same time, Miss Landless was seized with an instinctive hostility towards Jasper, who, she thought, was unduly menacing Rosa Bud. Matters between the two young men were smoothed over to some extent, and on the following Christmas Eve, John Jasper decided to bring them together at a convivial gathering in his own house.

On December 23rd Jasper visited the Opium Den in London. Next day he returned to Cloisterham, and was followed thither by the Opium Woman, who had heard him use threatening language in his sleep towards someone called "Ned" (Jasper's nickname for Edwin Drood).

At night (Christmas Eve) the three men met and dined. It was a night of wild storm. The next morning Jasper hastened to Canon Crisparkle's house shouting excitedly that his dear nephew had disappeared, and that he was convinced he had been murdered.

He plainly indicated that he believed the murderer was Neville Landless, in whose company Drood had left Jasper's house at midnight; and Neville Landless was apprehended, but subsequently released for want of evidence.

On December 26th Mr. Grewgious visited Jasper and informed him that the engagement between Drood and Miss Bud had been broken off. It is in evidence that on hearing this news for the first time, Jasper "gasped, tore his hair, shrieked" and finally swooned away.

Shortly afterwards Canon Crisparkle visiting the Weir on the river, discovered Edwin Drood's watch and chain, which had been placed in the timbers; and in a pool below he found Drood's scarf-pin.

It is in evidence that the accused, Jasper, after a short interval, renewed his attentions to Miss Rosa Bud, and exercised so great a terror upon her that she deemed it advisable to take refuge in London under the supervision of Mr. Grewgious and her friend Miss Twinkleton. Neville Landless also removed to London, where he was visited by his sister Helena.

Meanwhile, a careful watch was kept upon John Jasper by a "stranger," known as Dick Datchery. This person took lodgings opposite Jasper's house and had him under close observation. "Datchery" (which is admittedly an assumed name) interviewed several persons, including Durdles and "Princess Puffer," and kept a private record in chalk marks of all facts thus ascertained. In consequence of the suspicions excited by these circumstances, a warrant was applied for and John Jasper was arrested on a charge of Wilful Murder.

To this he pleads "NOT GUILTY," and this is the issue to be tried.

The following WITNESSES will be called:

ANTHONY DURDLES	}	By Counsel for the Prosecution.
CANON CRISPARKLE		
HELENA LANDLESS		
"PRINCESS PUFFER"	}	By Counsel for the Defence.
[THOMAS] BAZZARD		

NOTE

The design on the front page of this Indictment is a reproduction of that on the wrapper of the monthly parts of "The Mystery of Edwin Drood" as originally issued in 1870. It was drawn by Charles Allston Collins, and has been the cause of much controversy and speculation.

CONDITIONS AGREED UPON BETWEEN THE PROSECUTION AND DEFENCE

The three formal witnesses (that is to say, Crisparkle and Durdles for the Prosecution and the Opium Woman for the Defence) shall not in their evidence-in-chief go beyond the book or make any statements not expressly made therein, but in cross-examination they may, in response to specific questions, give explanations not expressly contained in the book.

The two chief witnesses (that is to say, Helena Landless for the Prosecution and Bazzard for the Defence) shall be free both in examination-in-chief and in cross-examination to make statements not made in the book, provided that they are not contradicted therein.

All statements made in the book shall be taken to be true and admitted by both sides, and any statement by a witness contradicting such statements shall be considered thereby proved to be false.

The said two chief witnesses (and no others) shall be allowed to give hearsay evidence.

The Defence having agreed not to call Edwin Drood, the Prosecution agree not to comment upon his absence from the witness-box either in speech or cross-examination, but the Prosecution reserve the right to comment upon the silence of Edwin Drood subsequent to the murder.

Both sides having agreed not to call Grewgious, it is agreed that neither side shall comment upon the fact that the other has not called him.

The Defence agree that the legal point that no conviction can take place since no body has been found, shall be raised only after the retirement of the jury, but the Defence reserves the right to comment upon the absence of a body as part of the general absence of direct evidence of the commission of a murder.

REPORT OF THE PROCEEDINGS

His Lordship having taken his seat, the Prisoner was immediately put into the dock, and addressed by the Clerk of Arraigns in the following terms:

John Jasper, the charge against you is that you did feloniously, wilfully, and with malice aforethought, kill your nephew, Edwin Drood, in the City of Cloisterham, on the night of the 24th of December, 1860. Are you guilty, or not guilty?

THE PRISONER: Not guilty.

THE CLERK OF ARRAIGNS: Will the gentlemen of the Jury please rise, and sit down as I call their names? Mr. George Bernard Shaw, Sir Edward Russell, Dr. W. L. Courtney, Mr. W. W. Jacobs, Mr. Pett Ridge, Mr. Tom Gallon, Mr. Max Pemberton, Mr. Coulson Kernahan, Mr. Edwin Pugh, Mr. William de Morgan, Mr. Arthur Morrison, Mr. Francesco Berger, Mr. Ridgwell Cullum, Mr. Justin Huntly McCarthy, Mr. William Archer, Mr. Thomas Seccombe— you shall well and truly try the Prisoner at the Bar, John Jasper, for the murder of Edwin Drood, and a true verdict give according to the evidence.

Mr. George Bernard Shaw was elected Foreman.

MR. WALTERS: I appear for the prosecution, my Lord.

JUDGE: Mr. Cuming Walters, I think, for the prosecution. Is there anyone with you?

MR. MATZ: I am with him, my Lord.

MR. CECIL CHESTERTON: I appear for the defence, my Lord.

JUDGE: Mr. Chesterton, I think, for the defence. One s, I think. Is anyone with you?

MR. CROTCH: I am, my Lord.

[THE CASE FOR THE PROSECUTION.]

Mr. Matz then proceeded to open the case for the prosecution in the following speech:

MY LORD AND GENTLEMEN OF THE JURY—

The case to be tried is one of murder—murder which we shall contend was premeditated, pre-arranged and carried out in a methodical and determined manner.

The Prisoner is John Jasper, Lay Precentor at Cloisterham Cathedral. The Prosecution will set itself to prove that on the night of the 24th December he murdered in that city his nephew Edwin Drood, an Engineer.

The said Edwin Drood was 21 years of age, and for some years was betrothed to Miss Rosa Bud in fulfilment of a dying wish of their respective parents (now deceased).

To this young lady the Prisoner acted as music master, and admittedly was enamoured of her, although he kept this fact secret from Edwin Drood.

On the evening in question—the 24th December—Edwin Drood and Neville Landless—a pupil of the Revd. Septimus Crisparkle—dined together with the Prisoner in his rooms in the Gate House adjoining the Cathedral.

The night was a terribly stormy one. After leaving the Prisoner, some time about midnight, the two young men took a walk to the river to see the effect of the storm on the water, and returned to the house of the Revd. Septimus Crisparkle in Minor Canon Corner. Here Edwin Drood left his companion, intending to return to his Uncle's lodgings.

Nothing has been heard or seen of him since.

Gentlemen, it is our painful duty to produce evidence to prove that Edwin Drood was murdered by his Uncle, the Prisoner. We contend that Jasper divested him of his watch and chain and his scarf pin, articles the Prisoner had, on another occasion, explained to the local jeweller he knew Drood to possess. The words he used were that he had "an inventory of them in his mind."

We contend that Jasper then cast the body of his victim into a vault in the Cathedral precincts, the key of which, or a duplicate, he had previously become possessed of. There had also been placed in the vicinity a quantity of quicklime, and we submit that Jasper, having made some inquiries into its properties, used this for the purpose of removing all traces of the body in the shortest period of time. We submit that he got rid of the watch and chain and scarf pin in the river, either in the hope of disposing of material which the quicklime would not destroy, or to give the impression, should they be found, that the young man was drowned.

We shall in evidence show that the Prisoner had *motive* for his crime, that he made elaborate preparations for its enactment, and that he succeeded in his terrible deed.

The evidence may be circumstantial only. But circumstantial evidence, I submit, may be extremely strong—as strong indeed as any direct evidence.

We shall show you that all the acts of John Jasper for some time previous to the committal of his atrocious crime were self-incriminatory. Not merely that, but they exhibit his mind working out the very means by which that crime was to be committed. *After* his terrible deed was accomplished, his actions, to those who observed him closely, also indicated clearly his guilt.

The Prisoner, having made up his mind that, for his own selfish ends Edwin Drood must be killed, first chose the spot best suited to his purpose, and laid methodical plans to secure access to that spot. He paid visits to it in the company of one, Durdles, the Cloisterham stonemason, whom he drugged with doctored wine whilst there, in order that he might acquire secretly the key to a certain vault. He knew where quicklime could be procured without loss of time. He interviewed other persons, and timed the hour and everything else so thoroughly that nothing essential for his purpose was overlooked.

Now, gentlemen, it is necessary to refer briefly to some further facts bearing upon the history of this crime.

Neville Landless, upon whom Jasper cast suspicion of being the murderer, and his sister Helena, were both students in Cloisterham: the brother, a pupil of the Revd. Septimus Crisparkle, and the sister a pupil at Miss Twinkleton's Academy in the city. They came from Ceylon, where they had been severely ill-treated, and had made several attempts to escape. On each occasion of the flight Helena "dressed as a boy and showed the daring of a man." Neville, a highly strung and emotional youth, took immediate objection to Drood because of his "air of proprietorship" over Rosa; whilst Helena instinctively disliked Jasper because she saw that he loved Rosa and that Rosa feared him. It is worth noting as a significant fact that at the earliest stage Rosa appealed to Helena for aid and every assistance was promised to her.

A slight quarrel between Edwin Drood and Neville Landless took place in Jasper's rooms, and undoubtedly Jasper goaded them on by his taunts. On this occasion Jasper gave them some mulled wine which had taken him a long time to mix and compound. They drank to the toast proposed by Jasper and their speech quickly became thick and indistinct, indicating that there was a sinister design in the mixing and compounding. Drood became boastful, and Neville Landless resented his tone, and at the height of the dispute, flung the dregs of his wine at Edwin Drood. Although posing as a Peacemaker Jasper actually fomented the hostility of these two young men. He seemed to delight in it and it enabled him subsequently to report to Crisparkle that Neville was "*murderous*." Indeed he went so far as to assert that he "might have laid his dear boy at his feet, and that it was no fault of his that he did not."

The Revd. Mr. Crisparkle talked with Helena and Neville on the latter's rash conduct, and he expressed extreme regret and promised to exercise more caution in future. On another occasion Crisparkle visited Jasper, who read to him passages from his diary expressing fears for Drood's safety. A few days later Drood, at the suggestion of Jasper, wrote and agreed to dine with him and Neville on Christmas Eve at the Gate house, Cloisterham—in order that the two young men should become friends. Their walk after dinner is evidence that this object was fully achieved.

We submit that, the whole plans having thus been prepared, the murder of Edwin Drood took place after the parting of the young men, and that John Jasper and no other was the murderer. In support of this we shall produce evidence to prove that Jasper acted in a highly incriminatory manner.

The next morning whilst great commotion was raging in the vicinity of the cathedral over the damage done by the storm, John Jasper broke into the crowd crying: "Where is my nephew?" as if everybody knew he was missing, whereas no one but the prisoner had any reason to think he was not in the Prisoner's rooms. He even volunteered the statement that Drood had gone "down to the river last night, with *Mr. Neville*, to look at the storm, and had not been back?" and demanded that Mr. Neville should be called.

These utterances were made to the Revd. Canon, and showed clearly that the murderer felt so confident that he had executed his deed with perfect thoroughness that no fear of discovery need enter his mind. But knowing his nephew was murdered he tried immediately to fix the deed upon another.

I must direct your attention to one other matter. John Jasper, whether guilty or not of murder, is indisputably a hypocrite, leading a double life. Like most criminals he was also capable of foolish mistakes. Had he not killed his "dear boy," as he called him, he would have made investigations of his whereabouts, he would have refrained from courting inquiries, and would not have excited the hostility of Rosa Bud.

But, gentlemen, most criminals of the John Jasper type, make at least one error in the execution of their crime, which ultimately finds them out. Jasper made his. Having as I have said, divested Edwin Drood of his watch and chain and scarf pin, all the jewellery he was aware Drood had upon his person, he felt safe. But he left, unknown to him, on the person of the young man a valuable gold ring set with rubies and diamonds, and this ring quicklime could not consume. The ring was once the property of Rosa Bud's mother and had been handed to Edwin Drood by Mr. Grewgious, Rosa Bud's guardian, with strict instructions that he should give it to Rosa if he intended to marry her, or return it to Mr. Grewgious should Edwin and Rosa decide, as seemed likely, to break their betrothal.

This was a faithful promise and was witnessed by one, Bazzard, the clerk to the said Mr. Grewgious.

It so happened that on December 24th the young couple did break off their engagement. Therefore if Drood, by any chance, were now alive, that ring would have been returned to Mr. Grewgious, in accordance with his promise. But, gentlemen, it never has been returned, and why? We say because Drood is no longer alive, but dead, and that where the body was hidden after the murder, there that ring was hidden also.

Jasper knew of all the articles that were on the person of Edwin Drood, except that ring. He did not know of that because it had only been handed to Drood on the previous day.

Nor did Jasper know of the breaking off of the betrothal, else would there have been no object in his committing the murder. Evidence will be given that Drood promised Rosa he would not spoil his Uncle's Christmas festivities by telling him of their decision to part as lovers.

The first time Jasper learnt the fact was on the day following the murder, when he heard it from Mr. Grewgious. He then instantly "gasped, tore his hair, shrieked," swooned and "fell a heap of torn and miry clothes upon the floor." From this we infer that the information was unexpected and a shock to him.

Sometime afterwards the Revd. Canon Crisparkle found the watch and chain and scarf pin, when walking near the weir, and he will be called to give evidence on this and other facts.

Now, gentlemen, let me read to you an extract from the diary of Jasper entered after this discovery. It reads thus—

"My dear boy is murdered. The discovery of the watch and shirt pin convinces me that he was murdered on that night, and that his jewellery was taken from him to prevent identification by its means."

The word "murdered" was frequently in the mind of Jasper at this time, and he made use of it in several phrases in his diary, which clearly demonstrates that he was attempting to create the impression that his nephew was murdered, and, by using the words, hoped to divert attention from himself.

But he became so nervous of what he had written, that he declared to the Revd. Canon that he meant to "burn this year's diary at the year's end" and by so doing, as he evidently thought, destroy all evidence of his guilty conscience.

There is one more phase to touch upon.

It is admitted that John Jasper was secretly addicted to opium smoking and frequented a certain opium den in London kept by a person known as the "Princess Puffer." Whilst under the influence of opium he babbled strangely, moaned, and uttered significant words in the hearing of the opium woman. This woman followed him more than once to Cloisterham and on one of these occasions, the fateful 24th December, she accosted Edwin Drood, and for the price of three and sixpence offered to tell him something. He paid her the money and she asked him first his name, and when he told her Edwin, she wanted to know, "Is the short of that name Eddy?..." Drood answered "It is sometimes called so." "You be thankful your name is not *Ned*," she next replied, "because it is a threatened name: a dangerous name." "Threatened men live long," he assured her. Her reply was—

"Then Ned—so threatened is he, wherever he may be while I am a-talking to you, deary—should live to all eternity!"

Now, gentlemen, it is a striking and amazing fact that Jasper, and he only, called Edwin Drood "Ned"—the threatened name.

That very night Edwin Drood disappeared, and he has "never revisited the light of the sun."

A few months passed and no trace of the body of the ill-fated young man having been found, Jasper, feeling he had cleared his way effectively, called at the Nun's House (Miss Twinkleton's Academy) one afternoon in the vacation, and taking Rosa unawares made passionate love to her. On being repulsed he vowed vengeance on Neville Landless—the man against whom he had already directed suspicion. So horrified was Rosa, she flew for safety to her guardian Mr. Grewgious at Staple Inn. A strict watch was kept upon Jasper by a person calling himself Mr. Datchery, with the result that he was eventually arrested.

Gentlemen, that is the case put to you as briefly as possible—it is the case you have to try.

We feel confident that the evidence we shall place before you will convince you that the prisoner has committed a foul crime, and that we can safely leave the issue to you. Painful as your duty may be, we look to you to give your verdict faithfully and fearlessly in the interests of justice and your fellow-men.

THE FOREMAN: My Lord, one word. Did I understand the learned gentleman to say that he was going to call evidence?

MR. MATZ: Certainly.

THE FOREMAN: Well, then, all I can say is, that if the learned gentleman thinks the convictions of a British jury are going to be influenced by evidence, he little knows his fellow countrymen!

JUDGE: At the same time, in spite of this somewhat intemperate observation——[The remainder of his Lordship's words were inaudible.]

[EVIDENCE OF ANTHONY DURDLES.]

MR. MATZ: Call Anthony Durdles.

USHER: Anthony Durdles! [That gentleman immediately entered the witness-box.]

CLERK OF ARRAIGNS: The evidence that you shall give before the Court and Jury, shall be the truth, the whole truth, and nothing but the truth.

MR. WALTERS: Your name is Durdles?

WITNESS: Durdles is my name.

MR. WALTERS: Do you always call yourself Durdles?

WITNESS: I do; 'cause my name *is* Durdles.

MR. WALTERS: You are a stonemason, I believe?

WITNESS: Ay; Durdles is a stonemason.

MR. WALTERS: Would you mind telling us where you work?

WITNESS: Durdles works anywhere he can, up and down, round about the Cathedral.

MR. WALTERS: Round about the Cathedral. Thank you. Very good. Do you happen to know the prisoner, John Jasper?

WITNESS: Ay; I knows John Jarsper.

MR. WALTERS: And did you ever happen to meet him anywhere near the Cathedral?

WITNESS: Yes; Durdles met Mister Jarsper near the Cathedral.

MR. WALTERS: Perhaps you met him more than once?

WITNESS: Twice.

MR. WALTERS: You met him twice. What did you go with him to the Cathedral for?

WITNESS: Well, sir; he——

MR. WALTERS: Yes: speak up, please.

JUDGE: I must interpose. The witness cannot possibly know what Mr. Jasper went to the Cathedral for.

MR. WALTERS: My Lord, with respectful submission to you, the prisoner might have told him.

JUDGE: But for that purpose you must examine the prisoner in chief.

MR. WALTERS: I think, my Lord, that you will find a conversation took place between Durdles and the prisoner, and that I am perfectly justified in asking what the conversation was.

JUDGE: Yes; I think so.

MR. WALTERS (*to witness*): Let us know what the conversation was between you and Mr. Jasper.

WITNESS: He says to me, "Is there anything new in the crypt?" and I says, "Anything new! Anything old, you mean."

MR. WALTERS: Yes?

WITNESS: Yes.

MR. WALTERS: What happened then?

WITNESS: We went down in the crypt, and he give me a drink out of his bottle. Fine stuff it was, too.

MR. WALTERS: And what about that bundle which I believe you carried?

WITNESS: He asked me if he could carry my bundle.

MR. WALTERS: Yes?

WITNESS: Ay.

MR. WALTERS: What was in your bundle?

WITNESS: Durdles knows what was in his bundle. Keys, among other things.

MR. WALTERS: Oh, keys. And I suppose you let him carry your bundle?

WITNESS: I did. Well, I had another drink out of his bottle.

MR. WALTERS: Did you happen on that occasion to see any quicklime lying about?

WITNESS: Well, there's always quicklime lying about the crypt. Always.

MR. WALTERS: You noticed it. Did Jasper happen to notice it?

WITNESS: He did. He asked me what it was for.

MR. WALTERS: Oh, he asked you what it was for. And did you tell him?

WITNESS: Yes; I told him it 'ud burn anything; burn your boots, and with a little handy stirring, it 'ud burn your bones.

MR. WALTERS: It would burn your bones with handy stirring. And when he put that curious question to you, did it occur to you there was a reason for it?

WITNESS: Durdles thinks everybody 'as a reason for everything they says and does.

MR. WALTERS: When he asked you would that quicklime burn, you thought he must have a reason for it?

WITNESS: Yes; so I did.

MR. WALTERS: People use quicklime for quite innocent purposes, I believe, don't they?

WITNESS: Yes.

MR. WALTERS: They use it for cement?

WITNESS: Yes.

MR. WALTERS: What else do they use it for?

WITNESS: Bodies.

MR. WALTERS: Did you think, by the way he was making his inquiries, that he wanted to know if it would burn something else besides ordinary stuff?

WITNESS: I didn't think as 'ow he wanted a heap of quicklime to burn his waste paper with.

MR. WALTERS: What happened next? You had a drink out of the bottle, and you had a little talk: what happened then? Did you go home?

WITNESS: No; I fell asleep.

MR. WALTERS: Oh, you fell asleep?

WITNESS: Yes.

MR. WALTERS: Anything else?

WITNESS: I had a dream.

MR. WALTERS: You had a dream before you woke up?

WITNESS: Yes.

MR. WALTERS: What was the nature of that dream?

WITNESS: I dreamt that Mister Jarsper was a-moving around me, handling my keys, and I thought I was left alone in the dark. Then I see a light coming back, and then I found Mr. Jarsper waking me up, saying "Hi! wake up!"

MR. WALTERS: Did you wake up?

WITNESS: Yes.

MR. WALTERS: Did you remember how long you had been asleep?

WITNESS: A long time. I remember the clock struck two.

MR. WALTERS: And you went in about midnight?

WITNESS: Yes.

MR. WALTERS: You had two hours' sleep?

WITNESS: Yes, I suppose so.

MR. WALTERS: Anything else? Did you notice anything?

WITNESS: When I woke up, I sees my key on the ground, and I says, "I dropped you, did I?" So I picks it up, and asks Mister Jarsper for my bundle.

MR. WALTERS: Did he give it to you?

WITNESS: Yes.

MR. WALTERS: I think you had on that occasion a little conversation about a curious art of yours—tapping the tombs?

WITNESS: Yes; oh, yes—yes.

MR. WALTERS: Would you mind telling the court?

WITNESS: I told him, with my little hammer I could tap and go on tapping, and I could tell whether anything was solid or whether it was hollow. For instance, I says, "Tap, tap, old 'un crumbled up in stone coffin in the vault!"

MR. WALTERS: That's what you said, is it?

WITNESS: Yes.

MR. WALTERS: And what did Mr. Jasper say to that?

WITNESS: He said it was wonderful, and I says, "No; I ain't going to take it as a gift, 'cause it's all out o' my own head."

MR. WALTERS: I understand you told him what you could do by tapping the walls—tell whether it was hollow or solid?

WITNESS: Yes, Durdles can tell whether it's hollow or solid by its tap.

MR. WALTERS: Was he interested in your conversation?

WITNESS: Very much, sir.

MR. WALTERS: Did you happen to notice the Sapsea tomb?

WITNESS: Durdles knows the Sapsea tomb.

MR. WALTERS: There is only one body in that tomb at present?

WITNESS: Yes.

MR. WALTERS: Did you tap the Sapsea tomb with your hammer, and did it sound surprising there?

WITNESS: It sounded more solid than usual.

MR. WALTERS: Since then, you have tapped it lately, and it sounds a little more solid?

WITNESS: Yes.

MR. CHESTERTON: This is contrary to an understanding. This is a formal witness, not to be cross-examined.

MR. WALTERS: Very well, I will go on. (*To witness.*) Did you meet him at another time?

MR. CHESTERTON: This is only formal evidence.

JUDGE: What is the point?

MR. CHESTERTON: You will find before you, my Lord, a document, and you will find there that certain witnesses who are to be cross-examined at length will be free to go beyond certain admitted evidence. The formal witnesses are not to do so.

JUDGE (*after perusing the "Conditions"*): Yes, I think I take your point, Mr. Chesterman—or Chesterton—whatever it is. The point, I understand, is that you are cross-examining this witness as if he were a principal witness of the trial.

MR. CHESTERTON: In the second paragraph I think you will notice——

MR. WALTERS: It is not of great importance to me.

JUDGE: One moment: I will see. (*After reading the paragraph referred to.*) I think you are justified up to the point to which you have gone, but I should recommend you to terminate it with some rapidity.

MR. WALTERS: I only want to ask one question. (*To witness.*) You did have a conversation with Mr. Datchery?

WITNESS: Yes.

MR. CHESTERTON: I ask you to say, my Lord, that the Jury must entirely disregard the statement about the tapping.

THE FOREMAN: How are we to dismiss it from our minds, my Lord? It is a very difficult point.

MR. WALTERS: I think I shall leave the Jury to draw their own conclusions. All I want to know from Durdles is, did he have a conversation with Datchery?

WITNESS: Yes.

MR. WALTERS: Thank you. That is all.

WITNESS: Thank you, sir. I'll drink your health on the way home, p'raps twice, and I won't go home till morning.

[DURDLES CROSS-EXAMINED.]

MR. CROTCH: One moment, please.

WITNESS: Oh, beg pardon, sir, beg pardon.

MR. CROTCH: Now, Durdles, you know all about the destructive qualities of quicklime?

WITNESS: Yes.

MR. CROTCH: Do you say that quicklime will not destroy metals?

WITNESS: No; I don't think quicklime will destroy metals.

MR. CROTCH: You don't think it will?

WITNESS: No, I knows it won't.

MR. CROTCH: Now, Durdles——

JUDGE: I must ask you to address the witness in more respectful terms, such as "Mr." Durdles.

MR. CROTCH: Very well, my Lord.

WITNESS: *Mister* Durdles, sir.

MR. CROTCH (*to witness*): I understand you were employed round about the Cathedral, and that you know all about the crypt?

WITNESS: Yes, sir.

MR. CROTCH: Now, tell me what was the state of the windows in 1860.

WITNESS: Ay?

MR. CROTCH: I put it to you again. In what state were the windows of the crypt in 1860?

WITNESS: Do you mean clean or dirty?

MR. CROTCH: I put it to you they were in a very broken condition?

WITNESS: Yes, sir; always broken.

MR. CROTCH: As a matter of fact, they were not only broken, weren't they, but partially boarded up?

WITNESS: Well, I can't remember, sir.

MR. CROTCH: Can't remember! You were constantly in the crypt!

WITNESS: Some of 'em.

MR. CROTCH: How many windows are there?

WITNESS: I don't know.

MR. WALTERS: I don't suppose the witness is expected to count windows!

WITNESS: Thank you, sir.

MR. CROTCH: Well, now, Mr. Durdles, I will ask you another question. As a matter of fact, have you not on many occasions chased little boys and others out of the crypt?

WITNESS: Yes, and they've chased me.

MR. CROTCH: Where did these boys find their way into the crypt?

WITNESS: Ay?

MR. CROTCH: You don't know?

WITNESS: No, I don't.

MR. CROTCH: You swear you don't know?

WITNESS: Ay, I swear I don't know.

MR. CROTCH: You have never seen them creeping through the windows of the crypt?

WITNESS: Might be; when I've been sober.

MR. CROTCH: That'll do. Now, you tell us that you met Mr. Datchery. Is that so?

WITNESS: Yes.

MR. CROTCH: Have you ever admitted Mr. Datchery to the Sapsea vault?

MR. WALTERS: This is going far beyond—

MR. CHESTERTON: If my learned friend will look at the first paragraph he will see that in cross-examination the formal witnesses may, in response to specific questions, give explanations not expressly contained in the book.

MR. WALTERS: Then I must re-examine the witness.

MR. CHESTERTON: Certainly.

MR. CROTCH: Now, Mr. Durdles, have you ever admitted Mr. Datchery to the Sapsea vault?

WITNESS: Not that I can remember.

MR. CROTCH: If you cannot remember admitting Datchery, do you at any time remember admitting anybody else?

WITNESS: No; I can't say as I do.

MR. CROTCH: Thank you, Mr. Durdles.

MR. WALTERS: I won't trouble you to re-examine you, Mr. Durdles.

WITNESS: Well, good day. I'll drink your health on the way home, and I won't go home till morning—I beg your pardon, my Lord.

[EVIDENCE OF REVEREND CANON CRISPARKLE.]

MR. WALTERS: The Reverend Canon Crisparkle.

USHER: Reverend Canon Crisparkle.

[That gentleman responded to the call, and entering the witness box, was duly sworn.]

THE FOREMAN: May I interpose for a moment? This gentleman has been called as the Reverend Septimus Crisparkle. I submit to your Lordship that his real name is Christopher Nubbles, a man who was tried before you on the information of a certain Mr. Chuckster, on the charge of being a snob, and you, in one of those summings-up which have made your name famous wherever the English language is spoken, found that the charge brought by Mr. Chuckster was well and truly proved. Now, I contend that Mr. Christopher Nubbles has gone to Cloisterham, become a Minor Canon, taken the name of Crisparkle, and is here obviously a more intolerable snob than ever.

MR. WALTERS: Mr. Crisparkle; I believe you are a Minor Canon of Cloisterham Cathedral?

WITNESS: I am, sir.

MR. WALTERS: I believe your identity has never been disputed until this moment?

WITNESS: Never. I am glad to be able to answer that impertinent reflection.

MR. WALTERS: Do you happen to know John Jasper?

WITNESS: Very well. He was associated with me daily in the duties of the Cathedral.

MR. WALTERS: Did he ever tell you about his affection for his nephew, Edwin Drood?

WITNESS: Constantly.

MR. WALTERS: And did he, while in this confidential mood, also tell you of his great affection for Miss Rosa Bud?

WITNESS: No, I cannot charge my memory that he ever mentioned affection for her.

MR. WALTERS: Well, then, in that matter John Jasper deceived you?

WITNESS: Well, shall we say deceived? Guilty of a lapse of confidence to a priest. Theologically speaking it would be deceit, perhaps.

MR. WALTERS: I believe, Mr. Crisparkle, that you have been acting as tutor to Neville Landless?

WITNESS: Yes.

MR. WALTERS: Do you mind telling the court the opinion you formed of that man's character?

WITNESS: I should say a very impulsive man, but responsive to influence of any kind.

MR. WALTERS: I think he has a sister?

WITNESS: Oh, yes: Miss Helena Landless.

MR. WALTERS: Is he under her influence at all?

WITNESS: Yes, I should say she exercises a good and strong influence upon him.

JUDGE: I should suggest that question is very improper. We are all under the influence of each other to a great extent. I am as much under the influence of the foreman of the Jury that I almost entirely agree with the view that he takes of the situation when he mentions it. But I think it is not quite proper to say "Is he under the influence of his sister?" Surely?

MR. WALTERS: But, my Lord, this gentleman knows both parties, and is perfectly acquainted with their relationships.

WITNESS: Yes, well.

JUDGE: I——

MR. WALTERS: I will not press the point. I will ask you, Mr. Crisparkle, have you any influence?

WITNESS: Is that proper, my Lord?

JUDGE: Quite proper.

WITNESS: I should say I have done my best. I have talked to him from time to time and found him very anxious to profit by any words I was able to say.

MR. WALTERS: You said he was impetuous. Perhaps he has one or two little faults of that sort. Would you regard them as dangerous?

WITNESS: No, no; oh no. The faults of an undisciplined boy.

MR. WALTERS: Has he any good qualities?

WITNESS: Many, which appear to me to far outweigh the others.

MR. WALTERS: Suppose Neville Landless had a little quarrel with another young man. Would you attach much importance to it?

WITNESS: No, I think not: very little, I think. Hot-tempered youth—soon over. He would be the first to regret it.

MR. WALTERS: Did you know Edwin Drood?

WITNESS: Yes.

MR. WALTERS: And you heard of a quarrel between him and Neville Landless?

WITNESS: Yes.

MR. WALTERS: Who told you about that quarrel?

WITNESS: Well, in the first instance, Neville Landless mentioned it to me when he came back to my house. He said he had made a bad beginning and was sorry. But immediately afterwards John Jasper came to the house, and gave me what I am bound to say was a very different account indeed.

MR. WALTERS: This is the John Jasper who had already deceived you?

WITNESS: Who had perhaps misled me by suppression.

MR. WALTERS: He was the John Jasper who was Edwin Drood's rival for Rosa Bud?

WITNESS: It would appear so.

MR. WALTERS: You say he gave a strong account of the quarrel—Is that correct?

WITNESS: It is more than correct. He said, when he came into the room, that he had had an awful time with him. I said, "Surely not as bad as that!" and he said "Murderous—murderous!"

MR. WALTERS: Are you sure he used the word "Murderous"?

WITNESS: I am absolutely certain.

MR. WALTERS: What did you say to that?

WITNESS: I said, "I must beg you not to use quite such strong language." He continued to use even stronger terms. He said there was something tigerish in Neville's blood. He was afraid he would have struck his dear boy, as he called him, down at his feet.

MR. WALTERS: You are quite sure those were his words?

WITNESS: Absolutely.

MR. WALTERS: And I suppose, following on that, you asked for an explanation from Neville? Did you have any conversation with him?

WITNESS: Yes, a long conversation with him in company with his sister.

MR. WALTERS: Was Jasper satisfied with the explanation given to him?

WITNESS: No, I'm afraid not. A few days afterwards, when I was endeavouring to make peace between the two combatants, and arranged a meeting, Jasper took the opportunity to show me his diary, in which he had written his fears and suspicions in regard to his dear boy's safety.

MR. WALTERS: Fears and suspicions?

WITNESS: That was the phrase.

MR. WALTERS: May we take it then, that this man was always harping on danger and using the word "Murder," and influencing your mind against Neville Landless?

WITNESS: I am afraid that was the impression which I derived.

MR. WALTERS: Was that the impression left in your mind after the conversation with John Jasper?

WITNESS: Yes.

MR. WALTERS: I think you know that on the Christmas Eve following, there was a friendly little party?

WITNESS: Yes; I was instrumental in arranging it.

MR. WALTERS: Following on that, Neville Landless was, on the following day, to start on a walking expedition?

WITNESS: Yes.

MR. WALTERS: Did he tell you all about it?

WITNESS: Oh, yes.

MR. WALTERS: He was quite frank?

WITNESS: Quite frank.

MR. WALTERS: Did he start to carry out his plans?

WITNESS: He started.

MR. WALTERS: On the Christmas morning, early?

WITNESS: Yes.

MR. WALTERS: Do you remember that Christmas Eve?

WITNESS: Perfectly.

MR. WALTERS: Why?

WITNESS: Especially because of the beauty of Evensong that day. John Jasper was in splendid voice that day, and I congratulated him when he came out of the Cathedral. I said he must be in very good health.

MR. WALTERS: Very good health: did he say anything?

WITNESS: He said he *was* in very good health, and that the black humours were passing from him, and that he would have to burn his diary—consign it to the flames—that was the phrase.

MR. WALTERS: He also laughed?

WITNESS: He went laughing up the postern gate.

MR. WALTERS: Do you mind telling us whether laughing was common with John Jasper.

WITNESS: No.

MR. WALTERS: In short, you thought it an exceptional piece of good humour?

WITNESS: Yes; he made that impression on me.

MR. WALTERS: Do you remember what sort of night it was?

WITNESS: A terrible night of storm.

MR. WALTERS: Let us get on to the next morning. The next morning what happened?

WITNESS: Before I was about, while I was still in my dressing room, I was aware of a great noise at my gate, and there I saw John Jasper, insufficiently attired, crying very loudly to me in the house. I looked out, and asked what was the matter, and he said, "Where is my nephew?" Naturally, I said to him, "Why should you ask me?" and he said, "Last evening, very late, he went down to the river to see the storm, in company with Mr. Neville Landless," since when nothing had been heard of him. And then he said, "Call Mr. Neville." I told him Neville had already started.

MR. WALTERS: When this conversation took place between you and John Jasper, did it occur to you that he was dazed, as if suffering from the effect of drugs?

WITNESS: No.

MR. WALTERS: Did it strike you that he was particularly clear-headed?

WITNESS: I think so. Yes: he was very clear-headed.

MR. WALTERS: Was he concise and clear in his remarks?

WITNESS: Yes, perfectly clear.

MR. WALTERS: If anybody told you he was suffering from the effect of drugs, or was dazed or bewildered, would your observation bear that out?

WITNESS: No, indeed.

MR. WALTERS: What did you do in respect of Mr. Neville?

WITNESS: We sent some men after him, and Mr. Jasper and I followed. Directly we came up with him, Jasper said, "Where is my nephew?" and Neville said, "Why do you ask me?"

MR. WALTERS: What did Jasper say?

WITNESS: He said, "He was last seen in your company"—or words to that effect.

MR. WALTERS: When he said that, what sort of impression did it cause on you? What did you think it meant?

WITNESS: I am sorry to say I had the unpleasant impression that he meant to suggest that Neville Landless was in some way responsible for Drood's disappearance.

MR. WALTERS: Once more he was suggesting murder?

WITNESS: Yes, that was the impression.

MR. WALTERS: And once more suggesting that Neville Landless was the murderer?

WITNESS: That was so, undoubtedly.

MR. WALTERS: This man, Neville Landless, with this terrible charge hanging over him; did he come back readily?

WITNESS: Yes.

MR. WALTERS: Did he answer any questions put to him?

WITNESS: Quite frankly.

MR. WALTERS: Some time afterwards, you made a discovery, I think. Would you mind telling the Court what it was?

WITNESS: I was walking along by the river, some two miles above where these young men had gone for their walk—by the weir, in fact,—when I saw something shining brightly. Looking more closely, I thought it was a jewel. I immediately dived in, being fortunately a good swimmer, and found that it was a gold watch and chain. The chain was hanging on the timbers. Later I found in the mud a gold scarf-pin. The watch had the initials E. D. engraved on it.

MR. WALTERS: Did you tell Jasper you had discovered these things?

WITNESS: At once.

MR. WALTERS: Did he say anything about it?

WITNESS: Nothing at the time, but a few days later, when we were disrobing in the vestry, he showed me the diary to which I have alluded.

MR. WALTERS: Did it contain any reference to it?

WITNESS: I cannot charge my memory with the exact words, but something to this effect—"My poor boy is certainly murdered. The discovery of the watch and scarf-pin leaves that beyond doubt. They were no doubt thrown away to prevent identification of the body"—or words to that effect.

MR. WALTERS: One moment, Mr. Crisparkle. Am I right in saying that once more Murder was suggested to you?

WITNESS: Yes.

MR. WALTERS: And that Neville Landless was pointed to as the murderer?

WITNESS: Yes.

MR. WALTERS: And so that would be the impression left on your mind by your conversation with Jasper?

WITNESS: Yes.

MR. WALTERS: Whether it was right or wrong, that would be the impression left?

WITNESS: Whether right or wrong, that would undoubtedly be the impression.

MR. WALTERS: Thank you, Mr. Crisparkle.

THE FOREMAN: May I ask one question, my Lord?

JUDGE: Certainly.

THE FOREMAN: Do I understand the witness to say that the prisoner was a musician?

WITNESS: He was, my Lord.

FOREMAN: His case looks black indeed.

[CANON CRISPARKLE CROSS-EXAMINED.]

MR. CROTCH: Canon Crisparkle, you referred to the night of the preliminary quarrel and the return of Neville Landless. Do you remember accusing Neville of intoxication?

WITNESS: Quite well.

MR. CROTCH: You said, "You are not sober"?

WITNESS: I did so.

MR. CROTCH: Do you remember his reply?

WITNESS: He said, "Yes; I am afraid that is true, although I took very little to drink."

MR. CROTCH: "Although I can satisfy you at another time that I had very little to drink." I put it, those were the words he used?

WITNESS: Doubtless.

MR. CROTCH: You said you went down to the weir, which is two miles from the river?

WITNESS: No; two miles from the point at which Edwin Drood and Neville Landless went down to watch the storm. It is two miles higher up.

MR. CROTCH: And it was there you found the articles you have described?

WITNESS: That is so.

MR. CROTCH: What was the position of the watch and chain?

WITNESS: It was adhering to the timbers. Where two timbers crossed, it had become fixed.

MR. CROTCH: As though somebody had gone down with a hammer and nail and hung it up deliberately?

WITNESS: No, that I would not say.

MR. CROTCH: Was the pin in the mud?

WITNESS: In the mud.

MR. CROTCH: This was ordinary loose mud?

WITNESS: Yes, a kind of sludge.

MR. CROTCH: Did you find anything else?

WITNESS: No.

MR. CROTCH: Nothing else at all?

WITNESS: No.

MR. CROTCH: Now, Canon Crisparkle, I have just one question of some delicacy to ask. I hope you won't be offended. Is it not a fact that you are in love with Helena Landless?

MR. WALTERS: My lord, my lord, I must object. I think this is a secret to a man's breast, and my friend has no right to try to get it out.

WITNESS: My Lord, I have no objection to answer the question. The lady will appear before you shortly, and when you see her you will not be surprised that my heart is a little affected.

MR. CROTCH: Thank you, Canon Crisparkle.

MR. WALTERS: Canon Crisparkle, one word please, as to the exact position of the weir. I think you have not been carefully examining the exact position lately? You could not testify whether it was two miles, one mile, or one and a half miles, and would not commit yourself to an actual distance?

WITNESS: No; we are not in mathematics.

MR. WALTERS: If I told you it was a little nearer the Cathedral, you would not dispute it?

WITNESS: Not for a moment.

MR. WALTERS: Thank you, Canon Crisparkle. That will do.

[EVIDENCE OF HELENA LANDLESS.]

MR. WALTERS: Call Helena Landless.

USHER: Helena Landless!

[That lady was conducted to the witness-box, and duly sworn.]

MR. WALTERS: What is your name, please?

WITNESS: Helena Landless.

MR. WALTERS: And you have a brother named Neville?

WITNESS: Yes; a twin brother.

MR. WALTERS: Is there a great bond of sympathy between you and your brother?

WITNESS: A very great bond.

MR. WALTERS: Is it so strong that you have an intimate understanding of each other?

WITNESS: We almost know each other's thoughts.

MR. WALTERS: And I think you are accustomed to exercise influence on him—perhaps to lead him?

WITNESS: It always has been so.

MR. WALTERS: Where did you live when young?

WITNESS: In Ceylon.

MR. WALTERS: With your parents?

WITNESS: No. My parents died when we were young, and a step-father brought us up.

MR. WALTERS: How did he treat you?

WITNESS: Very badly indeed. He was always cruel and harsh to us.

MR. WALTERS: Ever beat you?

WITNESS: We were whipped like dogs, and we ran away.

MR. WALTERS: How old were you when you first ran away?

WITNESS: Seven.

MR. WALTERS: Who suggested running away?

WITNESS: I did.

MR. WALTERS: And did your brother follow you?

WITNESS: He always followed me.

MR. WALTERS: You planned everything?

WITNESS: I always planned.

MR. WALTERS: Weren't you afraid to run away?

WITNESS: I was afraid of nothing to be free.

MR. WALTERS: What did you do in order to make a flight successful?

WITNESS: I cut off my hair, and dressed myself as a boy.

MR. WALTERS: That needed a great amount of daring?

WITNESS: Well, the occasion needed all the daring I could command.

MR. WALTERS: And when it needs all the daring you can command, you don't mind daring?

WITNESS: No.

MR. WALTERS: As a matter of fact, you did it, I think, not only for yourself, but for your brother?

WITNESS: I think more for him than for myself.

MR. WALTERS: And you love your brother very much?

WITNESS: Dearly.

MR. WALTERS: Still?

WITNESS: Yes.

MR. WALTERS: Would you do as much again, Miss Landless?

WITNESS: I would; and more.

MR. WALTERS: As much for anybody else you love?

WITNESS: If I loved them dearly enough.

MR. WALTERS: You have lately come to England. When you came, tell us where you resided.

WITNESS: I went to Miss Twinkleton's at the Nun's House, and my brother went to Mr. Crisparkle's.

MR. WALTERS: I believe the Nun's House is an Academy?

WITNESS: Yes.

MR. WALTERS: Other girls there?

WITNESS: Yes, several.

MR. WALTERS: Miss Rosa Bud there?

WITNESS: Yes.

MR. WALTERS: Ever meet her?

WITNESS: Yes.

MR. WALTERS: Ever become friends with her?

WITNESS: Yes; very great friends.

MR. WALTERS: Did you form an estimate of her character?

WITNESS: I thought she was a sweet, lovable girl, but shy and timid.

MR. WALTERS: Not got your daring?

WITNESS: No.

MR. WALTERS: She was learning music, I think? Who was her tutor?

WITNESS: John Jasper.

MR. WALTERS: Do you remember a party at Canon Crisparkle's shortly after your arrival?

WITNESS: On the night of our arrival.

MR. WALTERS: Who was there?

WITNESS: Myself, Miss Twinkleton, and Rosa Bud, and Edwin Drood, and John Jasper.

MR. WALTERS: You are sure John Jasper was there?

WITNESS: Yes; I noticed him particularly.

MR. WALTERS: Why?

WITNESS: Because of his strange manner towards Rosa Bud.

MR. WALTERS: How?

WITNESS: He watched her closely. During the evening she sang to his accompaniment, and his eyes were fixed on her the whole time with a most peculiar expression, and this seemed to trouble Rosa, although she was not looking at him. Suddenly she covered her face with her hands, burst into tears, and said she was frightened and wanted to be taken away.

MR. WALTERS: You don't think it was pure imagination on her part? She was frightened?

WITNESS: Yes.

MR. WALTERS: When people are frightened there is danger about generally. Did you think there was any danger in his looking at her?

WITNESS: I thought there was danger in his looks.

MR. WALTERS: Did you ever speak to her about it?

WITNESS: Yes. She said she was terrified at him; that he haunted her like a ghost, and that he made secret love to her.

MR. WALTERS: And she didn't like it?

WITNESS: She begged me to take care of her, and stay with her.

MR. WALTERS: Did you promise to do so?

WITNESS: I said I would protect her.

MR. WALTERS: Be very careful. If this man frightened her, would he not equally frighten you?

WITNESS: In no circumstances.

MR. WALTERS: That is because you are a woman of daring?

WITNESS: I suppose so.

MR. WALTERS: If you promised to shield and protect her, you did not content yourself with words. Did you take any action?

WITNESS: I kept a sort of watch on John Jasper.

MR. WALTERS: Why on Jasper?

WITNESS: Because I felt that he menaced Rosa's peace and happiness.

MR. WALTERS: You thought he was the source of the danger?

WITNESS: No one but Jasper.

MR. WALTERS: Had she any enemies?

WITNESS: No; she was too sweet and lovable.

MR. WALTERS: And you thought it was John Jasper, and John Jasper alone?

WITNESS: Yes.

MR. WALTERS: We will leave that for a moment, and come to your brother. You are very intimate with your brother, and he confides in you. Were he and Drood friendly?

WITNESS: Yes, but they had a little misunderstanding.

MR. WALTERS: Misunderstanding?

WITNESS: Only a difference of opinion.

MR. WALTERS: Did you think it would lead your brother to make an attack on him?

WITNESS: The idea is preposterous.

MR. WALTERS: They had a quarrel at the outset?

WITNESS: My brother did not like the way in which Edwin Drood spoke of Rosa Bud. He thought he was too patronising. John Jasper came up, made a great deal more of it than it warranted, and then insisted on the young men going back with him to have a glass of wine—stirrup-cup, he called it.

MR. WALTERS: What was the effect on your brother?

WITNESS: Both became flushed and excited.

MR. WALTERS: Was it very usual with your brother?

WITNESS: No.

MR. WALTERS: Yet a small quantity had this effect on him. Did you suspect anything of the wine?

WITNESS: I am morally certain the wine was drugged.

MR. WALTERS: I believe after that there was to be a little patching up?

WITNESS: That was owing to Canon Crisparkle. They were all to meet and shake hands.

MR. WALTERS: Was it to be a large party, or confined to themselves?

WITNESS: Only my brother and Edwin Drood and John Jasper, who had invited them to his house.

MR. WALTERS: That was on the Christmas Eve?

WITNESS: Yes.

MR. WALTERS: Did you know anything about your brother's plans for the next day?

WITNESS: He had planned to go on a walking tour.

MR. WALTERS: You knew all about it?

WITNESS: Yes.

MR. WALTERS: All arranged?

WITNESS: Yes.

MR. WALTERS: No secret?

WITNESS: No.

MR. WALTERS: And to the best of your knowledge, he started on that tour next morning?

WITNESS: Yes.

MR. WALTERS: Now, to get back to the party: you saw your brother just before he went?

WITNESS: Yes.

MR. WALTERS: Was he happy and jolly going to the party?

WITNESS: No. He was ready to shake hands with Edwin Drood, but he had a strange dread of the gatehouse.

MR. WALTERS: He did not object to going?

WITNESS: No; because he wanted to shake hands with Edwin Drood.

MR. WALTERS: Then the main object of his going was, not to enjoy himself, but to shake hands with Edwin Drood?

WITNESS: Yes.

MR. WALTERS: And you think that was practically the only motive?

WITNESS: Yes.

MR. WALTERS: We are told that Neville was fetched back after starting on his journey.

WITNESS: Yes.

MR. WALTERS: Was it a surprise he was fetched back after Drood's extraordinary disappearance was mentioned?

WITNESS: It was.

MR. WALTERS: But when you heard who had fetched him back, was that a surprise?

WITNESS: No; because Jasper had always been his enemy from the first.

MR. WALTERS: You thought he had cast suspicion on him?

WITNESS: Jasper had hinted in Cloisterham to many people that if anything ever happened to his nephew my brother would be responsible for it.

MR. WALTERS: And so you knew that your brother was under deep suspicion when brought back to Cloisterham?

WITNESS: Yes.

MR. WALTERS: Did you take that very much to heart?

WITNESS: I did, indeed, seeing it concerned the one I loved best in the world.

MR. WALTERS: There were two persons you wanted to protect?

WITNESS: Yes.

MR. WALTERS: Who were they?

WITNESS: My brother, and Rosa Bud.

MR. WALTERS: You had a double motive, and you thought the danger came from one and the same man?

WITNESS: I certainly did.

MR. WALTERS: Who was that?

WITNESS: John Jasper.

MR. WALTERS: What did your brother do after all this?

WITNESS: He was so sad and unhappy that he left Cloisterham, and took lodgings in London.

MR. WALTERS: You went with him?

WITNESS: No, I stopped there to live it down.

MR. WALTERS: That is where your courage came in again?—But you need not reply. I shall leave it to the Jury to draw their own conclusions. And now, all this time you were watching Jasper? Did you discover anything about his actions?

WITNESS: Nothing definite.

MR. WALTERS: Did you hear of his going here and there?

WITNESS: Yes; there were periodical disappearances.

MR. WALTERS: Did you know where he went on those occasions?

WITNESS: Yes, he went to London.

MR. WALTERS: And when in Cloisterham, how did he behave?

WITNESS: He went about always throwing out hints that he had thought my brother so hot tempered that he was afraid for his nephew to meet him.

MR. WALTERS: Did he meet Rosa Bud again?

WITNESS: He made love to her.

MR. WALTERS: Did she receive him kindly?

WITNESS: Hated him, loathed him, was terrified at him.

MR. WALTERS: Did he say anything to her when he discovered what her attitude was?

WITNESS: He told her that nothing should prevent him from having her himself. No one should stand against him.

MR. WALTERS: Did he threaten anyone who did stand against him?

WITNESS: Yes; he threatened my brother's life.

MR. WALTERS: You mean, he said to Rosa Bud something which amounted to a threat against your brother's life?

WITNESS: He said he could place him in the greatest jeopardy and danger.

MR. WALTERS: Then you thought his danger would increase?

WITNESS: Yes.

MR. WALTERS: I suppose you went to London occasionally to see your brother?

WITNESS: Not often.

MR. WALTERS: Did you ever see Rosa Bud in London?

WITNESS: Yes. She fled to London, so terrified was she at Jasper with his desperate love-making. She went to Mr. Grewgious, her guardian.

MR. WALTERS: And you determined to shield her as much as possible?

WITNESS: More than ever.

MR. WALTERS: Did you ever recall those words, that you would not, in any circumstances, be afraid of Jasper?

WITNESS: Yes.

MR. WALTERS: Not a mere idle boast?

WITNESS: No.

MR. WALTERS: You meant it?

WITNESS: I did.

MR. WALTERS: Six months went by, and no progress made?

WITNESS: I found out nothing.

MR. WALTERS: Yet the danger remained, and increased?

WITNESS: I grew more and more anxious.

MR. WALTERS: It was the woman against the man, and the woman was making no headway?

WITNESS: Yes.

MR. WALTERS: Did you think it was about time to change your course of action?

WITNESS: I did.

MR. WALTERS: What did you do?

WITNESS: I remembered how, as a little girl, I dressed myself as a boy, and now I determined to dress myself as a man.

MR. WALTERS: That was the result of recalling what you had done as a girl?

WITNESS: Yes.

MR. WALTERS: What you had done in the past you could do again?

WITNESS: Yes.

MR. WALTERS: It was difficult, you realised?

WITNESS: Yes, it was difficult, but I determined to overcome every difficulty.

MR. WALTERS: You did not shrink?

WITNESS: Naturally I shrank, but the end was worth all the sacrifice.

MR. WALTERS: You determined to go through with it?

WITNESS: I did.

MR. WALTERS: Because you had this double motive?

WITNESS: That is so.

MR. WALTERS: The overpowering motive which overcame everything else?

WITNESS: Yes.

MR. WALTERS: Very well, now; if you could have avoided dressing yourself as a man, if some other course had been open to you, would you have taken it?

WITNESS: If I could have felt sure of success.

MR. WALTERS: But you felt this was the last resource, and determined to do it?

WITNESS: Yes.

MR. WALTERS: In order to appear as a man, you had to adopt a very complete disguise indeed. Did you remember what you did when you were a little girl? Did you cut off your hair again?

WITNESS: No, I thought I could manage.

MR. WALTERS: Miss Landless, I don't want to press you, but was there any particular, personal reason why you didn't wish to sacrifice your hair?

WITNESS: Am I obliged to answer that question?

JUDGE: No.

MR. WALTERS: His Lordship says you need not answer that question. I think we may leave it to the Jury, as human beings, to give their own answer. But, at all events, we understand that you did not cut off your hair. Did you whiten your eyebrows?

WITNESS: No.

MR. WALTERS: You thought you could manage?

WITNESS: I did.

MR. WALTERS: How did you disguise yourself effectively?

WITNESS: I put on a large wig of white hair.

MR. WALTERS: To conceal your own luxuriant tresses?

WITNESS: I bound them well down underneath.

MR. WALTERS: What else?

WITNESS: I thought, in keeping with a large head of white hair, I had better assume the free and easy manners of an elderly man, and I tried to put a little dash of swagger, and I wore a blue coat and buff waistcoat.

MR. WALTERS: It was not so difficult, after all, in some respects, for you are a rapid and fluent talker—you need not be shy, you are—and therefore, as Dick Datchery, the affable old gentleman, a bit garrulous, you did not find much difficulty?

WITNESS: No: I did not find it very difficult.

MR. WALTERS: What did you do in Cloisterham?

WITNESS: I put up at the Crozier Inn.

MR. WALTERS: Where is that?

WITNESS: In the High Street.

MR. WALTERS: Far from the Gate House?

WITNESS: No.

MR. WALTERS: Did you try the effect of your disguise on the people in the neighbourhood?

WITNESS: Yes, at the Crozier I walked in, asked a few questions, and ordered a man's dinner.

MR. WALTERS: You ordered a man's dinner?

WITNESS: You would not have had me ask for a glass of milk and a Sally Lunn!

JUDGE: What is a man's dinner?

WITNESS: I called for a fried sole, and a veal cutlet, and a pint of sherry. Something like a man's dinner!

MR. WALTERS: And did you consume this gargantuan feast?

WITNESS: I think you are an intelligent gentleman, and I will leave it to you.

MR. WALTERS: You may. Now let us come to your inquiries. I suppose you wanted lodgings?

WITNESS: I asked the waiter if he could direct me to any.

MR. WALTERS: And did he?

WITNESS: I asked for something old, architectural, and inconvenient.

MR. WALTERS: And he directed you?

WITNESS: He did.

MR. WALTERS: Very far?

WITNESS: No; not far: Mrs. Tope's house.

MR. WALTERS: Did you find it easily?

WITNESS: No. That would not have done. I wandered about a bit in the wrong direction, and inquired, and at last found it.

MR. WALTERS: The reason for all that?

WITNESS: I wanted to put everybody off the scent, and tried to act as to the manner born, so that if anybody were watching me they would really take me for the man I wanted to be.

MR. WALTERS: You thought it best to take every precaution, in case you were watched?

WITNESS: Yes.

MR. WALTERS: And they would think you had lost your way, and were a stranger?

WITNESS: Yes.

MR. WALTERS: As a matter of fact, you were not a stranger. Did you meet Mr. Jasper?

WITNESS: I made an excuse, and I went up and asked him if he could tell me anything as to the respectability of the Tope family.

MR. WALTERS: So that you bearded the lion in his den. Did he recognise you?

WITNESS: No; he did not know the mouse.

MR. WALTERS: There are other ways of detecting people than by appearance. Jasper is a musician with a very delicate ear. What about your voice?

WITNESS: Mr. Jasper had only heard it once, and that was months ago, and, besides, I can change it (*changing her voice*)—change the tone of my voice, and speak like a man.

MR. WALTERS: You can disguise it, Miss Landless, so that people would really think it was a man's voice?

WITNESS: Yes.

MR. WALTERS: Tell us what you discovered as to Mr. Jasper's movements at this time.

WITNESS: He absented himself from the Cathedral every now and then, and made periodical disappearances.

MR. WALTERS: Where did he go?

WITNESS: To London.

MR. WALTERS: Were you in correspondence with Mr. Grewgious, the family solicitor, in London?

WITNESS: Yes.

MR. WALTERS: Did he tell you he had seen Jasper?

WITNESS: Yes.

MR. WALTERS: So that, between you, you knew all about him?

WITNESS: Yes.

MR. WALTERS: In the character of Datchery, did you meet people?

WITNESS: Yes.

MR. WALTERS: Durdles?

WITNESS: Yes.

MR. WALTERS: The old opium woman?

WITNESS: Yes.

MR. WALTERS: Mr. Sapsea, the Mayor?

WITNESS: Yes.

MR. WALTERS: Did you talk to them familiarly?

WITNESS: Yes. I really knew their idiosyncrasies—everyone of them—so I fooled them to the top of their bent, and got everything out of them.

MR. WALTERS: I have no doubt but that you asked the old opium woman some questions?

WITNESS: She had been following Jasper to the Gate House, and she asked me, in a whisper, would I mind telling her who he was, his name, and where he lived.

MR. WALTERS: And you said it was John Jasper?

WITNESS: Yes. She asked, would I give her three-and-sixpence to buy some opium. She said that on Christmas Eve a young gentleman gave her three-and-sixpence, and he said that his name was Edwin. And she said where could she see Jasper? And I told her in the Cathedral.

MR. WALTERS: Did she go to the Cathedral next morning?

WITNESS: Yes; I saw her behind a pillar, shaking her fist at him.

MR. WALTERS: You think she knew something about him?

WITNESS: Yes; that she knew more about his character than anybody else suspected.

MR. WALTERS: May I take it that the results of your investigations led you to the conclusions about John Jasper—that they increased your suspicions?

WITNESS: I had my suspicions from the first.

MR. WALTERS: Did you keep a record of your successes at the time?

WITNESS: Yes.

MR. WALTERS: How?

WITNESS: In chalk marks.

MR. WALTERS: Why in chalk marks?

WITNESS: I like the old tavern way of keeping scores. You may make a little mark, and nobody but the scorer knows what it means: a small mark for a small success, and a big mark for a big one.

MR. WALTERS: Was another reason that you did not wish your woman's handwriting to be discovered?

WITNESS: That would never have done.

MR. WALTERS: Did you adopt any device to bring Jasper into your presence, or not?

WITNESS: Yes; Mr. Grewgious had told me that he had given a ring to Edwin Drood.

MR. WALTERS: And did you use that ring in any way?

WITNESS: Yes; it was this ring that I used to lure him.

MR. WALTERS: And then, when you confronted Jasper, you felt that you had sufficient to go upon to accuse him openly of murder?

WITNESS: I did. His appearance and agitation were sufficient.

MR. WALTERS: And so he was accused of murder; and your motives throughout were disinterested motives for the protection of Rosa Bud and your brother?

WITNESS: That is so.

MR. WALTERS: You knew Edwin Drood?

WITNESS: Yes.

MR. WALTERS: Do you think that if he had voluntarily disappeared while all this trouble was going on, he would have communicated with his friends?

WITNESS: Yes, he was a kind-hearted lad.

MR. WALTERS: You cannot understand him being silent while Rosa was in danger?

WITNESS: I am sure he would not be.

MR. WALTERS: You think that, wherever he was, he would have spoken, if alive?

WITNESS: I do.

MR. WALTERS: Thank you, that will do.

[HELENA LANDLESS CROSS-EXAMINED.]

MR. CHESTERTON: Miss Landless, you say you knew the prisoner to some extent before the disappearance of Edwin Drood?

WITNESS: Yes.

MR. CHESTERTON: When did you learn that the prisoner was addicted to opium smoking—or have you learned it?

WITNESS: Mr. Tope told me of a seizure he had in the Cathedral.

MR. CHESTERTON: When was that, approximately?

WITNESS: As far as I can remember, about a few weeks after I came to Cloisterham as Dick Datchery. Rosa told me how frightened she was of him after he had had a dream; that he used to go into a peculiar kind of dream, and a film came over his eyes, and then she was more terrified of him than before.

MR. CHESTERTON: But you are putting two very different dates. I want to know when you realised he was addicted to opium smoking.

WITNESS: It takes a little time to realise anything. We hear this and that, and we put two and two together.

MR. CHESTERTON: When Rosa gave you that information, did you suspect opium smoking?

WITNESS: I had a faint suspicion.

MR. CHESTERTON: It occurred to you that it was probably opium. You knew Edwin Drood, Miss Landless?

WITNESS: Yes.

MR. CHESTERTON: Was he a conspicuous person—a person to notice very much?

WITNESS: Not very much, with the exception of this: that he was rather patronising, and had the air of a lad who was very much at home with himself.

MR. CHESTERTON: He dressed like ordinary young men?

WITNESS: Yes.

MR. CHESTERTON: Wore trousers?

WITNESS: Yes, certainly, I believe so.

MR. CHESTERTON: Do you understand that the ring was found in the quicklime?

WITNESS: I believe so.

MR. CHESTERTON: Oh! you believe so!

WITNESS: It was found there.

MR. CHESTERTON: Were any buttons found there?

WITNESS: No, I believe not.

MR. CHESTERTON: I suppose Mr. Drood would presumably have on either a belt or braces. Was a buckle or a belt or braces found in the quicklime?

WITNESS: No.

MR. CHESTERTON: Nothing was found in the lime except this ring?

WITNESS: No.

MR. CHESTERTON: Thank you.

WITNESS: I could throw some light on that.

MR. CHESTERTON: Your Counsel will no doubt re-examine you. Now, I want to know about this disguise of yours. You told us that it was no new thing to disguise yourself, because you dressed up as a boy in Ceylon. Would you kindly tell me how old you were the last time you did it?

WITNESS: Thirteen.

MR. CHESTERTON: Do you really suggest that a little girl of thirteen dressing up as a little boy—dressing up as a boy of thirteen—is any sort of qualification for a young lady of 21 dressing up as an "old buffer living idly on his means"?

WITNESS: Yes; the girl is mother to the woman, as the boy is father to the man.

MR. CHESTERTON: Well, now, you have told us, Miss Landless, that in dressing up as Datchery, you wore a white wig, blue coat, buff waistcoat, and so on. Did you do anything to your face?

WITNESS: No.

MR. CHESTERTON: You did not paint your face at all?

WITNESS: I always have enough colour in my face without paint.

MR. CHESTERTON: You did not make up your face in any way?

WITNESS: No.

MR. CHESTERTON: Do you ask the Jury to believe that you had been going about Cloisterham as Helena Landless for more than six months—ever since you came to Canon Crisparkle's—that you had been going about as Miss Helena Landless; that you did not alter your face in any way, and went about as Dick Datchery, seeing the same people? Do you ask the Jury to believe that you were not recognised?

WITNESS: I ask them to believe it, because it is the truth.

MR. CHESTERTON: Very well; the Jury will decide that for themselves. You say you went to Cloisterham and put up at the Crozier?

WITNESS: Yes.

MR. CHESTERTON: You also told us that you ordered a certain meal—a fried sole, a veal cutlet, and a pint of sherry. When my learned friend asked you, you said you would leave it to us. I must ask you: did you consume that meal?

WITNESS: I am a healthy young woman, but I did not eat it all. I had a little of the fish, some of the cutlet, and some of the sherry.

MR. CHESTERTON: How much sherry?

WITNESS: I had a glass.

JUDGE: It is important to insist whether the glasses were ordinary wine glasses.

A JURYMAN (Mr. EDWIN PUGH): I think it is not a fair question.

JUDGE: Any question is fair that tends to bring out the truth. We have no reason to suppose that all the people in the Court are not lying—nay, even are not supporting fictitious characters!

THE JURYMAN: But a sherry glass might be a tumbler.

MR. CHESTERTON: Miss Landless, I press you. You say you only drank one glass. The remainder of the pint you left in the bottle.

WITNESS: I did not say that.

MR. CHESTERTON: What did you do?

WITNESS: If I must say, there were receptacles in the room used by smokers. Some went that way, some I left in the bottle, and some I drank.

MR. CHESTERTON: Were not people present?

WITNESS: Not all the time. Only part of the time.

MR. CHESTERTON: They retired simultaneously?

WITNESS: No; there were not many there when I went in. Some left at once; some finished their dinners and went away.

MR. CHESTERTON: And the fortunate moment arrived when you could pour out the sherry?

WITNESS: There are such things as fortunate moments.

MR. CHESTERTON: Your taste in food and drink interests me a little. I shall return to the Crozier. But later on, when staying at Tope's, you used to have an evening meal prepared for you, consisting of bread and cheese and salad and ale?

WITNESS: Yes.

MR. CHESTERTON: Was that the sort of meal you were accustomed to at Miss Twinkleton's?

WITNESS: But, you see, I was not at Miss Twinkleton's.

MR. CHESTERTON: But there would not have been anything eccentric about coffee or tea?

WITNESS: I think it would be a very feminine beverage.

MR. CHESTERTON: Very well. You told my learned friend that you did not really lose your way from the Crozier to Tope's?

WITNESS: Yes.

MR. CHESTERTON: The truth of your story you are prepared to stake on that being so?

WITNESS: Yes.

MR. CHESTERTON: Will the Jury look at page 191 of the book?[2] There it states "he soon became bewildered, and went boggling about and about the Cathedral tower, whenever he could catch a glimpse of it...." (*To the witness.*) You could catch a glimpse of it when you liked?

WITNESS: Yes.

MR. CHESTERTON: There was no question of catching a glimpse of it. You could go straight to it if you wanted to?

WITNESS: If you are quoting from the book.

MR. CHESTERTON: We are quoting from something that is admitted as evidence. Every statement made here must be taken as being true.

WITNESS: But that was a blind.

MR. CHESTERTON: I want to carry you further, Miss Landless—"with a general impression on his mind that Mrs. Tope's was somewhere very near it." Is that the general impression on your mind?

WITNESS: I knew exactly where to go to Mrs. Tope's.

MR. CHESTERTON: And this "general impression on your mind" goes on—"and that, like the children in the game of hot boiled beans and very good butter, he was warm in his search when he saw the tower, and cold when he didn't see it." Is not that a definite statement as to the condition of your mind, and not as to your external actions, and does it not assert that you did not know where Tope's lodgings were?

WITNESS: I take it as a blind.

JUDGE: I draw the attention of the Court to the fact that the conditions of anybody's frame of mind have been paid perhaps too little attention to, and if Miss Landless chooses to say that the original literary person from whom

I believe we procured most of this information was not quite accurate, one can only say she has probably gone outside the rules.

MR. CHESTERTON: My Lord, I would direct your attention to the third paragraph of the "Conditions."

JUDGE (*after perusing the paragraph referred to*): Yes, I see: that is, on the face of it, it is quite clear that a statement does appear to be made to that effect. The rest falls into the deplorable abyss of literature.

MR. CHESTERTON (*to witness*): Now, after you had been "boggling about" in search of a place which you knew perfectly well already, you met a small boy, I think?

WITNESS: I did.

MR. CHESTERTON: I need not trouble you with the conversation, but that boy agreed to conduct you to Tope's?

WITNESS: Yes.

MR. CHESTERTON: Now he brought you to a place from which the arched passage was visible?

WITNESS: Yes.

MR. CHESTERTON: And you said, "That's Tope's"?

WITNESS: Yes.

MR. CHESTERTON: And he answered, "Yer lie; it ain't. That's Jarsper's." Is that so?

WITNESS: Yes.

MR. CHESTERTON: And you said, "Indeed?" And you gave a "second look, of some interest." What was the meaning of that?

WITNESS: Well, of course, I knew it was Jasper's, but when Jasper's house or anything connected with him, was brought to my mind, I always thought it was interesting, and gave a look for that reason.

MR. CHESTERTON: But you knew you were going to Jasper's house?

WITNESS: Yes.

MR. CHESTERTON: But why did you give it a second look?

WITNESS: Because I was so interested.

MR. CHESTERTON: You knew it was Jasper's, because the boy said it was Jasper's, and you gave it "a look of some interest"!

WITNESS: We know that dinner is ready, but we look with interest at it before we sit down to it.

MR. CHESTERTON: You knew it was Jasper's, and gave "a second look of some interest" when told it was Jasper's. Now you went to Tope's, and you met, as you told us, Jasper and Mr. Sapsea, and other people. Now you kept your record, you told us, in chalk, and you told us that one of your reasons for doing that was that you must evade discovery of your handwriting?

WITNESS: That is so.

MR. CHESTERTON: Had it not been for the fact that you were a woman, I take it you ask us to believe that you would have written up in ordinary writing all that you thought and speculated about Jasper on the cupboard door?

WITNESS: I do not ask you to believe anything of the kind, for I should not have been so foolish. I could have written some words if I had wished to, but I would not write at all.

MR. CHESTERTON: You used the old tavern way of keeping scores. Where did you learn that?

WITNESS: In Ceylon.

MR. CHESTERTON: What is the Cingalese tavern way?

WITNESS: I have not been brought up in a drawing-room, but among a very rough set of people. My step-father was a low, common man, and frequented taverns, and we children could go inside and outside or anywhere.

MR. CHESTERTON: Are there taverns in Ceylon?

WITNESS: I don't know that they call them taverns.

MR. CHESTERTON: Do you suggest that the phrase "old tavern way of keeping scores" refers to Ceylon?

WITNESS: My chalk marks revert to the time when I was there.

MR. CHESTERTON: How did you keep scores in Ceylon?

WITNESS: I did not keep scores there, but I saw other people.

MR. CHESTERTON: How do you know how they were kept?

WITNESS: I did not say I did know exactly, but I learned that a little mark meant a certain quantity, a bigger mark more, and so on.

MR. CHESTERTON: You like the old tavern way of keeping scores, but do not know how it is done?

WITNESS: I know that a man that had quarts had large strokes, and a man that had pints smaller ones.

MR. CHESTERTON: You swear that was done in Ceylon?

WITNESS: I swear that sort of thing was done there.

MR. CHESTERTON: What sort of drinks do they have there?

WITNESS: I never had their drinks. I saw them drinking, but I did not know what it was. But I saw the scores being kept on the back of the door.

MR. CHESTERTON: Do you know what they were drinking at all?

WITNESS: I took it for spirits, and beer, and so on.

MR. CHESTERTON: So you knew little about the drinking, but a great deal about the scoring?

WITNESS: That interested me as a child. My brother and I used to talk about it.

MR. CHESTERTON: What was the purpose of the scores?

WITNESS: The tavern keepers would do it to know what was due from Tom Scott, or Jim Price.

MR. CHESTERTON: You told us that you undertook the Datchery impersonation, so to speak, in collaboration with Mr. Grewgious?

WITNESS: Yes.

MR. CHESTERTON: May I take it you know him well?

WITNESS: Yes.

MR. CHESTERTON: Frequently correspond with him?

WITNESS: I correspond with him.

MR. CHESTERTON: Receive letters from him?

WITNESS: I have had letters from him.

MR. CHESTERTON: You know his profession?

WITNESS: A lawyer.

MR. CHESTERTON: What sort?

WITNESS: I don't know.

JUDGE: He is a lawyer, and I think that covers it. He is, indeed, a particular kind of solicitor, but I think a lady might well be excused for not knowing that.

MR. WALTERS: A lawyer covers everything.

JUDGE: I think that is fair.

MR. CHESTERTON: What is he?

WITNESS: A lawyer.

MR. CHESTERTON: What sort of business does he carry on?

MR. WALTERS: She doesn't know.

MR. CHESTERTON: I submit she knows nothing about Mr. Grewgious, and that she has not had correspondence with him.

MR. WALTERS: The official record says she did know Mr. Grewgious, and saw him in his Chambers.

MR. CHESTERTON: She might know Mr. Grewgious, but have no correspondence with him. I am asking what sort of business he carries on.

WITNESS: I know he is a lawyer.

MR. CHESTERTON: And nothing more?

WITNESS: Women don't interest themselves very much in these things.

JUDGE: No, I think that's fair.

MR. CHESTERTON: Now, the next time we hear anything of the official records, Miss Landless, you were back again in London. How was that?—in your own proper person, and ceased to be Datchery.

WITNESS: I went up in the evening.

MR. CHESTERTON: In the evening?

WITNESS: By the last 'bus and train.

MR. CHESTERTON: What time?

WITNESS: The 'bus that leaves the Crozier.

MR. CHESTERTON: What time?

WITNESS: I forget exactly, but I think about six.

MR. CHESTERTON: Had you any reason for going up?

WITNESS: Yes.

MR. CHESTERTON: What was it?

WITNESS: I wanted to see my brother.

MR. CHESTERTON: There was no particular reason why that day more than any other day?

WITNESS: No, I think not.

MR. CHESTERTON: I suppose you will admit you were running a certain risk of discovery?

WITNESS: Yes, there was some, but I thought I should be able to avoid it.

MR. CHESTERTON: Anybody might follow you?

WITNESS: Might.

MR. CHESTERTON: You were a stranger in Cloisterham. Anybody might have followed you to London. You were running that risk for no particular reason at all?

WITNESS: Oh! but I knew my brother was very, very unhappy, and I knew I could cheer him and comfort him, and he was very, very dear to me.

MR. CHESTERTON: Your visit had nothing to do with Rosa's visit to London?

WITNESS: I did not know she was there.

MR. CHESTERTON: Mr. Grewgious had not written and asked you to go?

WITNESS: No.

MR. CHESTERTON: No reason?

WITNESS: Yes; the reason I have given you.

MR. CHESTERTON: But there was no particular reason?

WITNESS: Is it not particular to go and cheer one who is closely bound to you?

JUDGE: I think the witness's remark is quite clear. She says she had an impulse in an avowedly emotional atmosphere to go and see somebody.

MR. CHESTERTON: Very well. (*To witness.*) You met, you have told us, an opium woman?

WITNESS: Yes.

MR. CHESTERTON: And you had a conversation with her, and afterwards made a mark on your score—your Cingalese score?

WITNESS: Yes.

MR. CHESTERTON: A moderate mark; then you saw her, in the Cathedral, shake her fist at Jasper?

WITNESS: Yes.

MR. CHESTERTON: Then you made a big mark. What was the meaning of that?

MR. WALTERS: I am not sure that she is bound to answer that question. It is sufficient that she made the mark.

MR. CHESTERTON: I am endeavouring to show that this story is not true, as I shall represent to the Jury, and my motive for asking the question is, that I suggest it was not Miss Landless who made the mark. The witness who did make the mark will be summoned later, and asked why he made it.

WITNESS: You ask why I made the long mark?

MR. CHESTERTON: Yes.

WITNESS: Because I thought, when she shook her fist at Jasper, and putting with that the fact that she had followed him, I concluded that she knew something against him, and I thought I had scored, and scored heavily.

MR. CHESTERTON: Is that all?

WITNESS: I had learned more than that. I had learned that Edwin Drood had given her money for opium on Christmas Eve.

MR. CHESTERTON: What did that prove?

JUDGE: We must not go into what that could prove. The witness has given a perfectly clear and definite account of her proceedings, and I strongly suggest that unless there is some particular point to be made, she should now be released from the witness-box, because the other point whether she knows anything about the scoring at inns, or whether such practices are common in Ceylon, must be left to later discussion.

MR. CHESTERTON: That is not the point I am trying to make; but that there was no reason why she should make the score, and I asked why she made it. I believe she did not.

JUDGE: But if she replies that she makes long or short chalk marks, in accordance with the ebullitions of her emotional nature——

MR. CHESTERTON: She is entitled to do so.

JUDGE: That would be an answer, and the only answer to which you will be entitled at the moment.

MR. CHESTERTON: If she likes, she may.

JUDGE: She has told you that she made a long stroke because she thought she had made a great score in her own mind against Jasper, and that she made a shorter mark before because she had not made a big score. That is all that could be expected to be got out of her, without a self-contradiction which would amount to perjury.

MR. CHESTERTON: I have very little more to ask, and shall get through very quickly. (*To witness.*) Now, you tell us that your motives were very compelling. You didn't care much about Edwin Drood, did you?

WITNESS: No, there was nothing particular about him. I thought he was a nice young fellow.

MR. CHESTERTON: You did? You did not call him "base and trivial"?

WITNESS: When he acted as he did to my brother, I felt angry, and naturally said things I should not have said.

MR. CHESTERTON: Your feelings were not very strong?

WITNESS: No.

MR. CHESTERTON: Your motive, you say, was care for your brother and for Miss Rosa Bud?

WITNESS: That is so.

MR. CHESTERTON: Do you consider those motives adequate to induce you to take the course you say you took?

WITNESS: I do.

MR. CHESTERTON: Enough to make you take all risks?

WITNESS: Yes.

MR. CHESTERTON: To go all lengths?

WITNESS: To the risk of my life.

MR. CHESTERTON: Your life?

WITNESS: He was all I had.

MR. CHESTERTON: Enough to compel you to do anything?

WITNESS: Anything that was right and true. You can't catch me that way.

MR. CHESTERTON: I put it to you that the whole of your story is a romance.

WITNESS: You put it to me?

MR. CHESTERTON: I put it to you, in fairness.

WITNESS: Will you please consider that I am here on my oath?

MR. CHESTERTON (*to Judge*): Your Lordship knows I am bound to put that.

WITNESS: I can only answer that every word I have spoken is true.

MR. CHESTERTON: Suppose every word you have spoken is true: is there a single word you have spoken that proves that Edwin Drood was murdered?

WITNESS: I don't know that you have asked questions to elicit that.

MR. CHESTERTON: It is not my business. Is there a word in the whole of the testimony you have given to your own Counsel or to me that proves that Edwin Drood was murdered? Did you, for example, see Edwin Drood murdered?

WITNESS: No.

MR. CHESTERTON: Do you know anyone who saw the murder?

WITNESS: No.

MR. CHESTERTON: Have you seen his body?

WITNESS: No.

MR. CHESTERTON: Do you know anyone who has seen it?

WITNESS: I don't think his body could be seen.

MR. CHESTERTON: Then you really have no evidence to produce to prove that Edwin Drood is dead?

WITNESS: I have the ring.

MR. CHESTERTON: That is all the evidence—your whole case? I want to press this point very much. On that ring your case rests. Is that so?

WITNESS: I am not a woman who understands very much about legal proceedings. It is the first time I have been in court. It is a hard thing for a clever man like you to put a question like this to an unsophisticated witness.

MR. CHESTERTON: But you are the person who has worked out the whole scheme against Jasper. Does not the whole case for the death, not for the plan or the undertaking, but for the death having taken place, rest on the finding of that ring?

WITNESS: Well, perhaps the case for incriminating, bringing it home to Jasper, rests on the ring.

MR. CHESTERTON: And if that ring—the presence of that ring—could be satisfactorily explained—the presence of the ring in the quicklime could be satisfactorily explained in any other way—you would have nothing to produce to show that it was a murder?

WITNESS: I might have no evidence, but I should be morally certain.

MR. CHESTERTON: You would hold your opinion, we know, but you would have no evidence?

WITNESS: No.

JUDGE: I think we must be careful not to get into argument.

MR. CHESTERTON: My Lord, I am finishing.

WITNESS: What you and I think is evidence might be two different questions.

JUDGE: That is indeed very probable.

WITNESS: I don't think it fair to ask questions like that.

MR. CHESTERTON: I will take her answer.

MR. WALTERS (*re-examining*): It does not require particular affection for any particular person to wish that he should not be murdered?

WITNESS: No.

MR. WALTERS: Although you might not be violently enamoured of Edwin Drood, you might want to bring his murderer to justice?

WITNESS: Yes.

MR. WALTERS: It has been suggested that your story is entirely romance. If you had been acting a part, would you not naturally have been disgraced for ever in the eyes of all who know you?

WITNESS: I should indeed.

MR. WALTERS: Have you not a particular reason at present for wishing to stand high in the esteem of certain people?

WITNESS: I have.

MR. WALTERS: Don't you think you would forfeit that esteem if you stood there on your oath, and told a tissue of falsehoods?

WITNESS: I should.

MR. WALTERS: Is there not every reason why you should tell the truth?

WITNESS: There is.

MR. WALTERS: Have you anything to gain by telling lies?

WITNESS: I have all to lose.

MR. WALTERS: Have you not been working entirely for others throughout?

WITNESS: Yes.

MR. WALTERS: You would not have taken this part if you could have helped it?

WITNESS: No.

MR. WALTERS: And when you were making these investigations you did not want to go to everybody and ask his definite business—"What sort of lawyer are you?"?

WITNESS: No; I never thought about it. He was a lawyer, and that's all I knew.

MR. WALTERS: Have you ever written a tragedy that nobody will bring out?

WITNESS: No, indeed, I have not.

MR. WALTERS: And so you have no particular reason for standing in the limelight and making yourself a heroine. Thank you.

JUDGE: The Court will now adjourn for about ten or fifteen minutes.

The Court accordingly adjourned. On the resumption of the proceedings, Mr. Walters announced that the evidence of Miss Helena Landless had completed his case.

[THE CASE FOR THE DEFENCE.]

Mr. Crotch, in opening the case for the defence, said—

MY LORD, AND GENTLEMEN OF THE JURY—

I am not going to follow the example of my learned friend, but I am merely going to outline the defence as briefly as possible. I am going to say at once that we are not out to attempt to dispute in any way that the prisoner desired the death of Edwin Drood or that he intended to murder him, nor that he planned to murder him, nor that he actually attempted to murder him, nor indeed, my Lord, that at one time, and for some time, he did believe that he had actually murdered him. What we do say, however, is that no murder took place. For any murder there must be, not only a murderer, but a murdered man. Now, granted for a moment that in the prisoner at the bar you have a potential murderer, where is the murdered man?

MR. WALTERS: This is strictly against all agreements.

MR. CROTCH: I will put my statement in another way, my Lord.

MR. WALTERS: I draw your attention to this fact: it is agreed that the legal point that no conviction can take place since no body has been found, shall be raised only after the retirement of the jury. This ought not to have been introduced at all.

JUDGE: But we may assume, what is apparently the fact, that no murdered body has been found?

MR. WALTERS: But he went further, and said, "Where is the body?"

MR. CROTCH: May I placate my friend and say, have we a murdered man? We say John Jasper did not murder Edwin Drood on the Christmas Eve of 1860. We have every reason to believe that Edwin Drood is still alive, and in that case, of course, it follows that you cannot legally convict John Jasper for murder. Now, it will naturally be asked how, if a murder was admittedly attempted, it can have failed, and still more, that if it failed, how the supposed murderer could have believed that it had succeeded. Those questions will be probably solved: we hope they will be solved by the evidence which we shall put before you. All I think it is at the moment necessary to say is, that the key to the story will be found in the opium habits to which the prisoner undoubtedly was addicted. My Lord, there is a story told of an Irish priest, who, warning his congregation against the evils of intemperance, said, "What makes you shoot at your landlord?" And the reply came, "It's the drink." "And begad, what makes you fail to shoot him?" The same reply—"It's the drink." My Lord and Gentlemen of the Jury, we submit that, in a word, is the story of John Jasper. Now John Jasper is—presumably my friend will admit it—he has tried to prove it—I don't think he has demonstrated much by it—he has tried to get out of his witnesses that this man was an opium smoker. From our point of view that is excellent. We say that John Jasper had, on the night previous to this murderous attack on Edwin Drood, indulged in a gross opium debauch, and because he did, in the midst of the commission of his crime he had one of those sudden seizures to which he was subjected, and that under the influence of opium he failed to complete the crime, but still believed that he had. Because he was under the influence of opium, he completed it in imagination, and then afterwards imagined that he had completed it in fact; and because his victim—and this is the point that I want to draw your attention to especially—because his victim also was under the influence of opium, having been drugged by Jasper, he failed to give any connected or reasonable and rational account of what had happened in these circumstances. That, I submit, my Lord, and Gentlemen of the Jury, is the outline. The details will be presently filled in by witnesses, who will testify. You will perceive that if it is true—and we shall prove it to be true—then John Jasper, whatever his intention, however great his moral obliquity, cannot be legally convicted of murder.—Eliza Lascar, alias the "Princess Puffer."

[EVIDENCE OF THE "PRINCESS PUFFER."]

USHER: Eliza Lascar, alias "Princess Puffer"! [The witness entered the witness-box, and was duly sworn.]

MR. CROTCH: Are you sworn?

WITNESS: Yes, deary.

MR. CROTCH: Your name, I believe, is Eliza Lascar?

WITNESS: Yes, deary. Oh, my lungs is so weak!

MR. CROTCH: My dear lady!

WITNESS: Oh, my lungs!

MR. CROTCH: You are known as "Princess Puffer"?

WITNESS: Yes, deary. I got Heavens-hard drunk for sixteen year afore I took to this; but this don't hurt me, not to speak of.

MR. CROTCH: You keep an opium den in the East End of London, I believe?

WITNESS: I do; but business is slack.

MR. CROTCH: Do you know the prisoner?

WITNESS: Know him! Better far than all the Reverend Parsons put together know him.

MR. CROTCH: He is a customer of yours, I believe?

WITNESS: When he first came to me he was quite new to it, but after a while he could take his pipe with the best of 'em, deary.

MR. CROTCH: I conclude from that he was a heavy opium smoker?

WITNESS: He was, deary.

MR. CROTCH: Do you remember his being in your place on the night of the twelfth of December?

WITNESS: He was, deary. I see him coming to, and I says, deary, "Get him another ready when he wakes, and he will remember the market price of opium is very high."

MR. CROTCH: What was the date he next visited you?

WITNESS: December 23, my deary dear.

MR. CROTCH: You need not be so affectionate. What happened next day?

WITNESS: I followed him to his home.

MR. CROTCH: What happened?

WITNESS: I lost him where the omnibus he got into nigh his journey's end plies betwixt the station and the place.

MR. CROTCH: Did you meet anybody else?

WITNESS: I met a dear gentleman named Edwin.

MR. CROTCH: What did you say to him?

WITNESS: I said to him, "My lungs is weak, my lungs is bad"—and the dear gentleman he put three-and-sixpence in my hand.

MR. CROTCH: And when did you next meet the prisoner?

WITNESS: Oh, my poor head! In 1861. He comes to me all over like for the want of a smoke. I says, "You have come to the right place. This is the place where the all overs is smoked off."

MR. CROTCH: Then what happened?

WITNESS: Then what happened, deary? I follows him to Aldersgate Street, the place where he puts up, and I finds out where he comes from, and I says to my poor self "I missed you the first time, and I swore my oath I will not lose you again, my gentleman from Cloisterham. I'll go there first, and bide your coming." And I did. I goes to Cloisterham, and I waits outside the Nun's House, just where the omnibus goes, and he gets down, and I follows him up a bystreet till he disappears under a archway to the left. I turns round, and he was gone.

MR. CROTCH: Did you see any one?

WITNESS: A white-haired gentleman who told me that his name was Datchery.

MR. CROTCH: Did you go to the Cathedral next morning?

WITNESS: I did, deary.

MR. CROTCH: Did you see the prisoner there?

WITNESS: I see him from behind a pillar.

MR. CROTCH: You recognised him?

WITNESS: I recognised him, deary.

MR. CROTCH: Did you afterwards meet the white-haired gentleman you have spoken of?

WITNESS: I did, deary.

MR. CROTCH: Did you tell him you knew the prisoner?

WITNESS: I told him that I knew him.

MR. CROTCH: Yes?

WITNESS: I said, "I know him. I know him better than all the Reverend Parsons put together knows him."

MR. CROTCH: Thank you.

["PRINCESS PUFFER" CROSS-EXAMINED.]

MR. WALTERS: Just one question. When you met Edwin Drood, I think you told him "Ned" was a threatened name?

WITNESS: Yes, deary.

MR. WALTERS: What did you mean by "threatened"?

WITNESS: It was a bad name.

MR. WALTERS: Do you think a man threatened is in danger?

WITNESS: It sounds like it, deary, don't it?

MR. WALTERS: It does. I want you to agree with me. I think you were in the habit of listening to Mr. Jasper when he had a little opium?

WITNESS: That is so.

MR. WALTERS: Ever hear him say the word "Ned"?

WITNESS: I can't recollect. I should think he did.

MR. WALTERS: What made you hit upon the name "Ned" as a threatened name?

WITNESS: He talked about him in a very unkind way.

MR. WALTERS: You say the man threatened was in danger. Did you think "Ned" in danger?

WITNESS: I heard what he said. Shall I tell you?

MR. WALTERS: Not what he said. It doesn't matter. But I want to know that "Ned" was a threatened name.

WITNESS: That's right, deary.

MR. WALTERS: Were you giving warning to anybody of the name of "Ned"?

WITNESS: I told him it was a threatened name.

MR. WALTERS: Did you know he was called "Ned"?

WITNESS: I asked him.

MR. WALTERS: Did you know who called him "Ned"?

WITNESS: I don't know.

MR. WALTERS: If I told you that Jasper, and Jasper alone, called him "Ned"?

WITNESS: I should believe you, deary. I should believe you.

MR. WALTERS: And you would therefore also believe that Jasper was threatening him?

WITNESS: Yes, deary.

MR. WALTERS: And that he meant it?

WITNESS: Yes, deary.

MR. WALTERS: So you think there was murder in the mind of John Jasper?

WITNESS: I think he wanted to do him harm.

MR. WALTERS: Do you love John Jasper?

WITNESS: No, I don't.

MR. WALTERS: I suppose you don't love any of your customers?

WITNESS: I don't care much about 'em.

MR. WALTERS: But you don't turn them away? When they come to you you take their money?

WITNESS: Yes.

MR. WALTERS: Do you always follow your customers down to their private residences?

WITNESS: No.

MR. WALTERS: Why this one?

WITNESS: He had money.

MR. WALTERS: What! A poor man in a choir had got money?

WITNESS: He had money.

MR. WALTERS: It was worth all your while to go all the way to Cloisterham after one customer?

WITNESS: Yes.

MR. WALTERS: He had such a lot of money?

WITNESS: Yes; to me he had. I'm only a poor woman.

MR. WALTERS: He was richer than all your other customers?

WITNESS: Yes.

MR. WALTERS: You think so?

WITNESS: Yes.

MR. WALTERS: You don't know where all this money came from?

WITNESS: No.

MR. WALTERS: You hated him?

WITNESS: Yes.

MR. WALTERS: And you wanted his money?

WITNESS: Yes. He was always a-listening.

MR. WALTERS: I thought it was you listening?

WITNESS: Sometimes I would listen, and once he spoke to me of a hazardous journey, and he said, "I did it a hundred million times; I did it so often, that when it came to be really done, it was not worth the doing, it was done so soon, and when it comes to be real, it was so short that for the first time it seemed to be unreal. No struggle, no sign of danger, no consciousness of peril! I never dreamt that before." That's what he said, my deary dear.

MR. WALTERS: Well, he said, when it came to be done it was so short it was not worth doing?

WITNESS: He said it was not real for the first time.

MR. WALTERS: He talked about a real thing?

WITNESS: He says, deary, "When it comes to be real it seems to be unreal for the first time," my deary dear.

MR. WALTERS: He said, "when it comes to be real"?

WITNESS: "It seems unreal for the first time," my poppett.

MR. WALTERS: But when a man says "a real thing," he means a real thing?

MR. CHESTERTON: My Lord!

JUDGE: There is some element of paradox involved here. I cannot consent to allow the witness to be attacked merely because a criminal says that that which seemed real before it happened appeared unreal when it happened, because I suppose most of us in this room have committed crimes at some time or other, and that is a possible state of affairs.

MR. WALTERS: I will not ask any more questions, my Lord.

MR. CHESTERTON (*re-examining*): When you say that you imagined the prisoner was rich as compared with your other clients—they would be Chinamen and sailors and Lascars?

WITNESS: They was very poor, deary.

MR. CHESTERTON: He was a different class of man?

WITNESS: He was, my poppett.

MR. CHESTERTON: The other question I want to ask you is this: When you told Mr. Drood that "Ned" was a threatened name, what did Mr. Drood say?

WITNESS: He says, "But threatened men live long."

MR. CHESTERTON: What did you say?

WITNESS: "Then," I says to him, "Ned, so threatened is he, whoever he be, while I'm a talking to you, that he should live to all eternity."

MR. CHESTERTON: Thank you. Call Thomas Bazzard.

USHER: Thomas Bazzard!

[That gentleman entered the witness-box and was duly sworn.]

[EVIDENCE OF THOMAS BAZZARD.]

MR. CHESTERTON: Your name is Thomas Bazzard?

WITNESS: Yes.

MR. CHESTERTON: What is your profession?

WITNESS: I am a clerk and investigator to Mr. Grewgious, of Staple Inn.

MR. CHESTERTON: Mr. Grewgious is not, as he is wrongfully described I believe, in the indictment, a solicitor?

WITNESS: No; Mr. Grewgious is a member of the Bar, but is not practising. He is Receiver and Manager of two large estates.

MR. CHESTERTON: And what sort of work do you do?

WITNESS: I believe the work that I am at present engaged in is colloquially known as that of a "noser." That is to say, I am engaged partly in collecting the rents, and partly in inquiring what is going on with his tenants—whether they are stealing the game, and improperly dispersing the stock. Largely work of investigation outside the office.

MR. CHESTERTON: When did you enter his employment?

WITNESS: Ten years ago.

MR. CHESTERTON: Where were you born?

WITNESS: I am the son of a Norfolk farmer, I am sorry to say.

MR. CHESTERTON: If your employer said, "It would be extremely difficult to replace Mr. Bazzard," that would refer to your inquiry work?

WITNESS: I think that would refer to my inquiry work. Yes.

MR. CHESTERTON: Mr. Grewgious treats you rather respectfully?

WITNESS: Mr. Grewgious is extremely kind to me, and as he values my work outside, he allows a great deal of latitude as to my behaviour inside.

MR. CHESTERTON: Now, when did you first see Edwin Drood?

WITNESS: I think I saw him—by the way, I should like to point out that Mr. Grewgious was not the legal adviser to Edwin Drood.

MR. CHESTERTON: You might explain that to the Court.

WITNESS: I noticed in the copy of the Agreement that he was the legal adviser to Edwin Drood. So far as I know, that is not the case. I first saw him some time before Christmas 1860, at the office of Mr. Grewgious.

MR. CHESTERTON: Did Mr. Grewgious tell you about Mr. Drood's coming?

WITNESS: He did. Yes.

MR. CHESTERTON: And what was the general instruction that Mr. Grewgious gave you?

WITNESS: These instructions: he said he was going to have a private conversation—more or less private conversation—with Mr. Drood, and if I appeared to be very interested in it, it might embarrass Mr. Drood, and that therefore I should not pay any particular attention to it.

MR. CHESTERTON: What did you do?

WITNESS: What happened was this: I think we all had dinner, and then Mr. Grewgious had the private conversation in question. I understood that what happened was that he admonished Mr. Drood as to his proper feelings towards his future bride.

JUDGE: You did not hear that?

WITNESS: No; I didn't hear that. I took the opportunity to have a snooze. Waking up, Mr. Grewgious said to me, "I have handed a ring of diamonds and rubies to Mr. Drood." Mr. Drood handed a case and said, "You see?" I said, "I follow you both, sir, and I witness the transaction."

MR. CHESTERTON: What was the next occasion you saw him?

WITNESS: The next occasion I saw Mr. Edwin Drood was Jan. 1st, 1861.

MR. CHESTERTON: That was a week after you first met him?

WITNESS: Yes.

MR. CHESTERTON: Where did you meet him?

WITNESS: At a hotel in Holborn.

MR. CHESTERTON: Did you hear what happened to him after that?

WITNESS: After that, I was informed that he was very seriously ill with rheumatic fever, and was sent abroad to the South of France to get his health back.

MR. CHESTERTON: Did Mr. Grewgious ever tell you how he came across Edwin Drood?

WITNESS: What he told me was this: that on Christmas Eve, 1860, he received very late at night, a letter from Miss Rosa Bud, his ward, to whom he was very much attached, and, if I may be allowed to remark, to whose mother he was very devotedly attached also. This letter was written by Miss Bud immediately following her conversation with Mr. Edwin Drood, which is in the Official Record, I think, and it entreated Mr. Grewgious, in very strong terms, to be with her in Cloisterham on Christmas Day. The letter reached Mr. Grewgious very late in the evening, and owing to the defects of the railway system, some of which, I am glad to learn, have been altered since, it was impossible for Mr. Grewgious to get to Cloisterham except by posting down, which he accordingly did.

MR. CHESTERTON: There was no train after eight o'clock?

WITNESS: At that time no train after eight o'clock—from Victoria.

MR. CHESTERTON: He posted down, and what do you understand he did when he arrived at Cloisterham?

WITNESS: He told me that he drove into Cloisterham somewhere about 5.30. Passing the Postern Gate, he stopped his carriage, and asked it to wait a minute.

MR. CHESTERTON: Why?

WITNESS: He wanted to walk through the gate into the Churchyard, a few yards—some 40 or 50 yards, I think—in order to put some flowers on the grave of Miss Rosa Bud's mother, as I think it is stated in the official documents, he was very much attached to Miss Bud's mother.

MR. CHESTERTON: When he got there, whom did he find?

WITNESS: He found Edwin Drood lying prone.

MR. CHESTERTON: And what did he do?

WITNESS: I believe the first thing he did was to pick him up. He then shook him together, begged him to speak to him, and questioned him, and Edwin Drood entreated him to take him out of Cloisterham without any delay.

MR. CHESTERTON: I understand, Mr. Bazzard, from your narrative, that Mr. Drood could give practically no coherent account of what had happened?

WITNESS: None whatever, beyond the fact that somebody had tried to strangle him, as he thought.

MR. CHESTERTON: When you saw him, what sort of memory had he of that night?

WITNESS: Vague and unsatisfactory.

MR. CHESTERTON: He could not have sworn that either Neville Landless or Jasper had attacked him?

WITNESS: He could not swear anything, except that he had been attacked.

MR. CHESTERTON: His sympathies leaned, of course, to Jasper rather than to Landless?

WITNESS: He was very loath indeed to think that his uncle, whom he had cherished with very great respect and esteem, had been concerned in the attempt to murder him.

MR. CHESTERTON: If he could have given evidence then, I take it he would have given evidence rather in favour of Jasper than of Landless?

WITNESS: That depends on the Jury.

JUDGE: I was going to remark that the question goes a little outside anything the witness is called upon to answer.

WITNESS: He was more inclined to——

THE FOREMAN: On this point the witness has made a very remarkable statement; that Mr. Grewgious shook Mr. Drood together. May I ask how many pieces Drood was in?

JUDGE: I think the question should be answered.

WITNESS: I was not there, my Lord, at the time. I merely repeat what Mr. Grewgious told me.

JUDGE: You attribute it to a violent metaphor on the part of Mr. Grewgious?

WITNESS: It is right that I should put the Jury in possession of all matters.

A JURYMAN (Mr. William Archer): May I ask where Mr. Grewgious is in the meantime? Met with a violent death?

MR. CHESTERTON: If the Jury will look at the Official Record——

THE FOREMAN: I am sorry to explain, my Lord, that all our documents have gone, covered with our autographs. (Further copies of the Official Documents were handed to the Jury by the Clerk of Arraigns.)

MR. CHESTERTON: If the Jury have the Document, they will see the last paragraph but one explains the matter. (*To Witness.*) You then saw Mr. Grewgious. What did Mr. Grewgious say?

WITNESS: What he said was this: that he personally very strongly suspected Jasper, but that Drood's recollections as to what happened on that evening were so confused and incoherent that any testimony he might have to give would not either clear Landless, or incriminate Jasper. He therefore said this: that if Landless were committed for trial it would be necessary to produce Drood, but failing that, he had better keep his continued existence a secret until matters had died down at Cloisterham, and until Jasper thought he was entirely secure.

MR. CHESTERTON: And therefore, what was Mr. Grewgious's plan?

WITNESS: His plan was this: that if I went down to Cloisterham prosecuting inquiries there, I should detect Jasper.

MR. CHESTERTON: And you did so?

WITNESS: I did so. Yes.

MR. CHESTERTON: When you went down, how did the case present itself to you as a problem?

WITNESS: I thought from what Mr. Grewgious told me about the case, that there were three cardinal mysteries. One was why Drood, if he had been murderously assaulted, could give no clear account, as to who had assaulted him; the second was why, if the prisoner was the author of that murderous assault, he had not effected it; and in the third place, why, having failed to kill Drood, he obviously thought he had killed him.

MR. CHESTERTON: Having put those three things to yourself, you went down to Cloisterham and disguised yourself?

WITNESS: I went to a costumier.

MR. CHESTERTON: You did not make up your face?

WITNESS: No.

MR. CHESTERTON: You were not known there?

WITNESS: As far as I know, no.

MR. CHESTERTON: But there might be an offchance, and so you put on a costume?

WITNESS: Yes.

MR. CHESTERTON: You went to the Crozier, and ordered a veal cutlet, a mutton chop, and a pint of sherry?

WITNESS: Yes—and I drank the sherry!

MR. CHESTERTON: And asked the waiter about lodgings?

WITNESS: I did.

MR. CHESTERTON: You asked for something Cathedrally?

WITNESS: I thought I ought to get something near the Cathedral, so as to be near to Jasper.

MR. CHESTERTON: They recommended you to Mr. Tope's?

WITNESS: They did.

MR. CHESTERTON: And you set out to go there?

WITNESS: I did.

MR. CHESTERTON: What happened?

WITNESS: I was told I should find the house on the right-hand side. It was so obvious that I went past it. I went on up a lane called Crow Lane, I believe, into the Vineries, and somewhere about there I met the boy named Deputy. I asked him to take me to Tope's, which he did.

MR. CHESTERTON: He took you to within sight, didn't he?

WITNESS: Yes; I beg pardon.

MR. CHESTERTON: He pointed out a window?

WITNESS: Yes.

MR. CHESTERTON: You said, "That's Tope's"?

WITNESS: Yes; I thought it was.

MR. CHESTERTON: He said it was Jasper's?

WITNESS: Yes; and I looked at it with some interest.

MR. CHESTERTON: You saw Jasper subsequently?

WITNESS: Yes.

MR. CHESTERTON: You called on him to inquire about the Tope's? You made that opportunity to call?

WITNESS: Yes.

MR. CHESTERTON: You walked about the Cathedral; met Sapsea and Durdles?

WITNESS: Yes.

MR. CHESTERTON: You met Deputy again?

WITNESS: Yes.

MR. CHESTERTON: And there was a conversation, I think, between you and Deputy, in which you said he was to take you to Durdles's house when you wished?

WITNESS: Yes.

MR. CHESTERTON: After you installed yourself in the Tope's lodgings, how did you propose to keep a record of your successes?

WITNESS: I rather amused myself by opening the cupboard door in my room, and chalking it up as is done in taverns which on occasions I have visited in Ceylon—I mean Norfolk.

MR. CHESTERTON: You were brought up as a boy in Norfolk?

WITNESS: Yes.

MR. CHESTERTON: And they keep chalk scores there?

WITNESS: They used to chalk it up by means of long or short lines.

MR. CHESTERTON: Generally according to the date of the week?

WITNESS: The big lines at the end of the week.

MR. CHESTERTON: You kept this record in this fashion?

WITNESS: Yes.

MR. CHESTERTON: Will you carry your mind back to one evening, I think in July, when Jasper came home comparatively late, and went under the archway, and passed up the staircase?

WITNESS: Yes.

MR. CHESTERTON: Do you remember an old woman following?

WITNESS: Yes.

MR. CHESTERTON: What passed between you?

WITNESS: I asked her if she was looking for anybody, and she, in substance, said that she would like to know the name and address of that gentleman. Then we had some further conversation, and she asked me, first of all for money for her lodgings, and then she asked for money for what she described as opium, which I gave her.

MR. CHESTERTON: She also mentioned an interview with a young gentleman on the previous Christmas Eve?

WITNESS: Yes, she told me she had been to Cloisterham before on Christmas Eve, and that she had met a youth named Ned, I think it was, who had also given her money. I took it she had been down on the same business as that night—following the prisoner.

MR. CHESTERTON: When you had done that, you went to your score?

WITNESS: When I had done that, I met Deputy, and he told me that "'Er Royal Highness the Princess Puffer" was staying at the Travellers' Tuppeny, and that she kept an opium den in the East End of London, and then I had very little doubt that that was the place from which she had followed the prisoner.

MR. CHESTERTON: You told her where she could see the prisoner next morning?

WITNESS: Yes.

MR. CHESTERTON: She saw him, and shook her fist at him?

WITNESS: She used dreadful language which is not even in the Official Records.

MR. CHESTERTON: When she came out, did you say to her, "Have you seen him?"?

WITNESS: I did.

MR. CHESTERTON: And did she say that she had seen him, and knew him better than all the Reverend Parsons put together?

WITNESS: Yes.

MR. CHESTERTON: You then went to the cupboard door, and what did you do?

WITNESS: I made a great score.

MR. CHESTERTON: What was its meaning?

WITNESS: That my interview with, and observations of the opium woman had settled the three main questions as to which I had gone down to Cloisterham to decide.

MR. CHESTERTON: Let us take them seriatim. First, how was it Drood——

WITNESS: From my conversation with her I gathered that Jasper took opium, and having opium, I had no doubt at all that he drugged Drood's wine, and that Drood was so affected as not to be able to give any clear account as to the event.

MR. CHESTERTON: The second question—How was it that, if the prisoner was the author of the assault, he had not achieved his purpose?

WITNESS: My views as to that also were clear. He had been at the opium den on the night before the Christmas Eve, when she last visited Cloisterham, and I have no doubt at all that he failed because he had an opium seizure— such a seizure as Mr. Grewgious saw him in, and as his nephew Drood saw him in.

MR. CHESTERTON: The third question—How came it, that having failed to kill Drood, he obviously thought he had done so?

WITNESS: That, I thought, was obvious, because he would have completed the murder in an opium trance, such a trance as, later, the "Princess Puffer" described to me, as Jasper having experienced inside the opium den.

MR. CHESTERTON: We have already heard from the "Princess Puffer" about its being unreal for the first time. That would fit in with your theory?

JUDGE: I am afraid the witness must have no theory. As soon as the examination has put its main point, we must go on.

MR. CHESTERTON (*to witness*): Then, did you get any confirmation of that view from Mr. Grewgious?

WITNESS: Yes, I wrote to Mr. Grewgious, and he told me of the seizure on Boxing Day—I think it was Boxing Day—when he had an interview with Jasper, the prisoner.

MR. CHESTERTON: And also did he tell you that Edwin Drood remembered his uncle in a seizure?

WITNESS: I remember that also.

MR. CHESTERTON: Did you gather that Drood had had his wine drugged on a previous occasion?

WITNESS: I gather that from the Official Records.

MR. CHESTERTON: Then, did you claim your promise from Deputy?

WITNESS: I did.

MR. CHESTERTON: We have been told in evidence that a ring was put in the crypt.

WITNESS: Yes?

MR. CHESTERTON: Does that surprise you?

WITNESS: Not in the least.

MR. CHESTERTON: Why?

WITNESS: Because I put it there.

MR. CHESTERTON: What was your object in pursuing that course?

WITNESS: This was the ring, I may say, that I had seen pass from Mr. Grewgious to Drood, of the existence of which, I may perhaps point out, it is obvious from the study of the Official Records, Jasper knew nothing at all; and acting under instructions from Mr. Grewgious, who had received the ring back from Drood, I obtained with the assistance of my friend Durdles access to the Sapsea vault, and therein I placed the ring. My object in doing that was, that subsequently, when Mr. Grewgious offered a reward for the discovery of the ring, the prisoner could be entrapped into a visit to the vault.

MR. CHESTERTON: I take it, Mr. Grewgious would plaster Cloisterham with the description of the ring as believed to be on the person of Edwin Drood?

WITNESS: That is what he did.

MR. CHESTERTON: It would be a large placard?

WITNESS: Yes.

MR. CHESTERTON: Rather like this? (*Handing to the witness a reproduction of the original cover design for the book.*)

WITNESS: Very like the second illustration from the top on the left-hand side.

MR. CHESTERTON: Very well: that was your plan—that Jasper should be caught taking the ring, and thus be convicted of attempted murder?

WITNESS: Quite.

MR. CHESTERTON: Of which you believed him to be guilty?

WITNESS: Beyond doubt.

MR. CHESTERTON: It is not my business to ask you what happened, but I suppose somehow or other he got arrested for actual murder. Is that correct?

WITNESS: Quite right.

MR. CHESTERTON: Thank you.

[THOMAS BAZZARD CROSS-EXAMINED.]

MR. WALTERS (*cross-examining*): I think you have said several times that you come from Norfolk?

WITNESS: I was born in Norfolk.

MR. WALTERS: Is that the country where the dumplings come from?

WITNESS: Some, no doubt.

MR. WALTERS: Where you come from also!

WITNESS: Yes.

MR. WALTERS: Curious coincidence! You are a farmer's son?

WITNESS: Yes.

MR. WALTERS: And very ambitious?

WITNESS: I have not said so.

MR. WALTERS: Don't you want to get on?

WITNESS: I don't think that is very ambitious. I think being very ambitious is more than wanting to get on.

MR. WALTERS: In order to get on you came to London from Norfolk?

WITNESS: A good many people have done that before, I am afraid.

MR. WALTERS: You wanted to give London the benefit of any genius you had?

WITNESS: Thank you very much indeed. I wanted to be usefully employed.

MR. WALTERS: And you became professionally engaged to Mr. Grewgious?

WITNESS: Yes.

MR. WALTERS: And you occupied the responsible and honourable position of "Noser"?

WITNESS: Quite right. The best position I could get.

MR. WALTERS: And he treated you with great respect?

WITNESS: Yes.

MR. WALTERS: Remarkable respect from a barrister to his clerk?

WITNESS: That is due to the fact that he is a man of exceptional graciousness.

MR. WALTERS: And you treated him with great respect?

WITNESS: I worked for him, I think, very hard, and with very great fidelity.

MR. WALTERS: I said you treated him with great respect. I did not ask about your fidelity.

WITNESS: You will forgive my mentioning it, won't you?

MR. WALTERS: Now do you mind replying to the question? You treated him with very great respect?

WITNESS: I hope so.

MR. WALTERS: If you ever gave him a surly answer, would that be respectful?

WITNESS: I don't know. It would depend on the degree of surliness.

MR. WALTERS: And you took his money as a good and faithful servant?

WITNESS: I hope so.

MR. WALTERS: And were absolutely devoted to his interests?

WITNESS: I hope so.

MR. WALTERS: So that on one occasion you fell asleep while he was talking?

WITNESS: Yes; but in pursuance to his instructions. He told me that a conversation was going to take place which was no affair of mine, and that he was not particularly anxious for me to overhear it. But he was very anxious that I should witness the transaction at the end of the conversation.

MR. WALTERS: Would it not have been more respectful to walk out of the room?

WITNESS: I think not. It would place him in an extremely awkward position.

MR. WALTERS: You preferred to fall asleep and snore?

WITNESS: May I answer? If I had gone out, Mr. Grewgious would have had to come for me, and to have told Edwin Drood that he required a witness.

MR. WALTERS: You preferred to fall asleep and snore in the presence of a client?

WITNESS: I had forty winks after dinner.

MR. WALTERS: You had forty winks, as you call it, while your employer was engaged with an important client?

WITNESS: In a conversation which I was not supposed to hear.

MR. WALTERS: Do you frequently fall asleep?

WITNESS: No; I have no desire to slumber at present.

MR. WALTERS: No; I think we shall wake you up presently. Do you usually sleep when respectable clients enter your office?

WITNESS: No; I don't usually receive such instructions.

MR. WALTERS: That was the only respectful way of treating your master and client?

WITNESS: I have had no remonstrance from Mr. Grewgious for it. I am still in his employment. He thought it was worth his while to go on employing me.

MR. WALTERS: Mr. Bazzard, the story you have told proves to me that you have rather a strong imagination. Am I right?

WITNESS: If it proves it to you, my good sir, by all means. I prefer to answer questions.

MR. WALTERS: But probably you have also convinced the Jury that you are a gentleman of some imagination?

WITNESS: It's not for me to say—only to tender my evidence.

MR. WALTERS: I believe you have written a Drama?

WITNESS: Once, many years ago, when a young man, I did write a Tragedy. A dreadful admission! I hope no other witness whose veracity is challenged——

MR. WALTERS: What was the name of that Tragedy?

WITNESS: It is "The Thorn of Anxiety."

MR. WALTERS: Has it ever come out?

WITNESS: No.

MR. WALTERS: It is, I suppose, a work of great genius?

WITNESS: I should not like to say.

MR. WALTERS: But all plays are!

WITNESS: Do you think so! If you would like to read it, I should be delighted.

MR. WALTERS: I don't wish you to be modest. Dramatists usually are not. I suppose there are such things as good dramas and bad dramas?

WITNESS: There are certainly bad dramas.

MR. WALTERS: Just to give us your opinion: do you think yours was good or bad?

WITNESS: I don't know. I am naturally impressed in its favour, but several people—some people to whom I submitted it—they rather doubt it.

MR. WALTERS: They don't think there is any "Magic" in it?

WITNESS: No.

MR. WALTERS: I don't want you to think for a moment that all dramatists are bad people. I only mean that you may possibly have written a bad drama.

WITNESS: There are several dramatists on the Jury, and they can take their impression.

MR. WALTERS: You would not give a reason why it has not come out?

WITNESS: I don't think it is up to me. If I am asked for a reason, one is I have had very little time to push its merits.

MR. WALTERS: I suppose though, that even bad plays are produced sometimes?

WITNESS: No doubt.

MR. WALTERS: It's not only the bad ones, though, that are accepted?

WITNESS: No.

MR. WALTERS: It must be a bad play that does not get accepted in these days? When a man of genius such as you——

WITNESS: Please; if you don't mind.

JUDGE: It is not in evidence that this man is a genius.

THE FOREMAN: I respectfully submit that it is in evidence that he has written a play.

JUDGE: Very true.

MR. WALTERS: When a man of your ability, of some little ambition, cannot get his play accepted, he sometimes resorts to other means—other than the ordinary means?

WITNESS: I could not tell you. I have only tried the ordinary.

MR. WALTERS: You are a legal gentleman?

WITNESS: No, sir.

MR. WALTERS: You are connected with the law?

WITNESS: No, sir.

MR. WALTERS: Not connected with a lawyer?

WITNESS: No, sir.

MR. WALTERS: Know nothing about the law?

WITNESS: I wouldn't say that. I thought all Englishmen were supposed to understand the Statutes under which they live. I am in the office of a barrister who is not acting as a barrister, but as Receiver and Manager of two large estates.

MR. WALTERS: And therefore no lawyer.

WITNESS: It is not for me to say that.

MR. WALTERS: Do you think you can give a straightforward answer to any plain question?

WITNESS: I think I have done so.

MR. WALTERS: You have probably heard that unsuccessful authors and dramatists, when they cannot get their plays or books accepted by ordinary means, adopt little devices?

WITNESS: I don't think I have.

MR. WALTERS: You have never heard of an actress losing her jewels, or an author pretending to commit suicide?

WITNESS: I have heard of them actually doing it.

MR. WALTERS: Ever heard of an author saying he has been to the North Pole, and writing a book? Would it not be absolutely providential if something occurred to you to bring you into notoriety?

WITNESS: No.

MR. WALTERS: It would not relieve your "Thorn of Anxiety"?

WITNESS: No.

MR. WALTERS: In other words, would it not rather be to your advantage to be talked about as a hero.

WITNESS: I have never seriously considered the proposition.

MR. WALTERS: You are rather fond of theatricals, are you not?

WITNESS: No, sir.

MR. WALTERS: Fond of the Drama?

WITNESS: I am rather too busy to be interested in it. As I have told you, I am too busy——

MR. WALTERS: Yes or no?

WITNESS: You ought to take my answer. I say I have been too engaged in looking after my livelihood to take a lively interest in the British Drama.

MR. WALTERS: You do take an interest?

WITNESS: Yes.

MR. WALTERS: Does your employer know it?

WITNESS: Yes.

MR. WALTERS: He has seen your play?

WITNESS: Yes.

MR. WALTERS: It rather interested him?

WITNESS: I think what interested him was my work for him.

MR. WALTERS: He is a keen man, you know.

WITNESS: I know. I can tell you he is not interested in the Drama.

MR. WALTERS: You have a few friends who are interested in the Drama? Do you meet a few fellow Dramatists?

WITNESS: No, sir.

MR. WALTERS: But it is in the Official Records that you do!

WITNESS: Then, I must be wrong, and I do. I was told to answer "yes or no." I meet a few people who are interested in the Drama, having attempted plays as I have. I meet them at rather long but happy intervals.

MR. WALTERS: I suppose they would like their plays produced?

WITNESS: I dare say.

MR. WALTERS: Once more I ask you—and do please give a straightforward answer—

WITNESS: With great respect, I very much resent that.

MR. WALTERS: Do you think it would be to your advantage to be a little famous?

JUDGE: I must interpose, because I don't think I know any human being in the world who would not think it to his advantage to be rather famous. Also I must remind the Court that two speeches have to be made on both sides, and we are all in high hopes of hanging somebody, and it really ought to be abbreviated if possible. I don't think anyone can say that the answers of the present witness have been such as in any way to expose him to discredit, but if the barrister examining desires to ask a few more questions, by all means let him do so, and then I think we should pass on as quickly as possible.

WITNESS: I could achieve very great notoriety if I were hanged.

JUDGE: Yes: live in hopes.

MR. WALTERS (continuing his cross-examination): Datchery is rather a famous person at present?

WITNESS: Yes.

MR. WALTERS: And I suppose you consider it an honour to be considered Datchery?

WITNESS: I am proud to have worked down there.

MR. WALTERS: You knew a little about the Drood case?

WITNESS: Yes.

MR. WALTERS: You knew a little of it from Mr. Grewgious?

WITNESS: I have stated that it was Mr. Grewgious's idea that I should go down there and investigate in character.

MR. WALTERS: It was not a dramatic inspiration?

WITNESS: The inspiration was Mr. Grewgious's.

MR. WALTERS: When you fell asleep on that occasion, were you pretending?

WITNESS: No.

MR. WALTERS: You were not preparing for the part of Datchery in advance?

WITNESS: Datchery never snored, did he?

MR. WALTERS: You were not preparing a part?

WITNESS: I had no idea that Mr. Drood was going to be murdered.

MR. WALTERS: You were not pretending, therefore?

WITNESS: I was not.

MR. WALTERS: You are a man of short sentences, according to the Official Record?

WITNESS: Yes.

MR. WALTERS: Very abrupt?

WITNESS: Yes.

MR. WALTERS: Have you given us only two or three words to-night in your sentences?

WITNESS: I have been answering under some provocation.

MR. WALTERS: Did your Counsel provoke you to your long sentences?

WITNESS: I trust not.

MR. WALTERS: Were you pretending when you gave those short sentences in Mr. Datchery's character?

WITNESS: No; but a man in the witness-box is not a good criterion.

MR. WALTERS: I suppose you can write?

WITNESS: Yes.

MR. WALTERS: I suppose your professional standing teaches you to keep correct records?

WITNESS: Yes.

MR. WALTERS: You did not keep the usual records making your investigations in Cloisterham?

WITNESS: What are the usual records?

MR. WALTERS: I put it to you that you did not write anything down?

WITNESS: I did.

MR. WALTERS: Why did you use the chalk marks?

WITNESS: Merely as a matter for my own amusement.

MR. WALTERS: Were they to be used in any way?

WITNESS: I should say not.

MR. WALTERS: You valued your time so much that you wasted it by putting chalk marks on a door!

WITNESS: The amount of time would not be much.

MR. WALTERS: You were not going to take the cupboard door to London as evidence?

WITNESS: No.

MR. WALTERS: It was all a waste of your time?

WITNESS: Yes; but harmless. Even a rejected dramatist is entitled to have some hobby.

MR. WALTERS: You know John Jasper?

WITNESS: Yes.

MR. WALTERS: Did you ever see him take opium?

WITNESS: Never.

MR. WALTERS: Do you know how long an opium fit lasts?

WITNESS: No. I imagine it rather depends on the amount of opium taken, and various other circumstances.

MR. WALTERS: Suppose a man was in the habit of having a particular smoke of opium—mixing it in a particular way; do you think it would be over in a few minutes?

WITNESS: I could not tell you. Nor do I know whether he had those habits.

MR. WALTERS: You don't think it would take a few hours?

WITNESS: No idea.

MR. WALTERS: Would it surprise you to know that after an orgy he would be clear-headed in the morning?

WITNESS: Nothing would surprise me, I think, from the little I have read of their literature.

MR. WALTERS: You know nothing about it?

WITNESS: As a matter of experience, that is the exhilarating fact.

MR. WALTERS: You never saw Jasper taking opium?

WITNESS: No.

MR. WALTERS: And you watched him in Cloisterham?

WITNESS: In the street. He never took any there.

MR. WALTERS: You believe that possibly he made a desperate attack on Edwin Drood?

WITNESS: Yes, I think so.

MR. WALTERS: He would possibly make an attack on someone else?

WITNESS: Yes.

MR. WALTERS: Don't you think, therefore, you were in some danger?

WITNESS: I don't think I was.

MR. WALTERS: You don't think you were in danger from a man who might make an attack? Are you a man of very great nerve?

WITNESS: It's not for me to say.

JUDGE: I don't think you have any right to ask him that. That is a matter of personal knowledge. It might be settled in a fight outside.

MR. WALTERS: One or two more questions. Have you a great affection for Edwin Drood?

WITNESS: I have not.

MR. WALTERS: Nor for Neville Landless?

WITNESS: No.

MR. WALTERS: No interest in Miss Helena Landless?

WITNESS: No.

MR. WALTERS: No interest whatever in any of the parties?

WITNESS: Business interest only.

MR. WALTERS: Then, why did you risk your valuable life?

WITNESS: In the first place, I don't think I exposed my life, valuable or otherwise, to any great risk. Why I went down there was because Mr. Grewgious asked me to do so, and because he had been a very generous and considerate employer to me, and I also thought that if I had good results he would reward me suitably.

MR. WALTERS: Can you give me any explanation, if Drood has disappeared, why he has not communicated with his friends?

JUDGE: That is surely a point for final discussion in abstract debate?

MR. WALTERS: I only ask if he can offer any explanation. (*To witness.*) Should you expect a man who has disappeared, and finding all his friends in danger, to communicate with his friends?

WITNESS: On that hypothetical case, I think I should. But that has no reference to the Drood question.

JUDGE: I think we should confine ourselves as sharply as we can to bringing out the actual facts, and not to abstract argument.

MR. WALTERS (*to witness*): Can you give us any reason why he should not communicate?

WITNESS: I cannot: but he has communicated with his friends.

MR. WALTERS: Are you going to produce any evidence?

WITNESS: That is in the hands of Counsel.

MR. WALTERS: Don't you think the white wig would give you away?

WITNESS: I can't tell you. I was in the hands of a costumier.

MR. WALTERS: You can go back to Norfolk, Mr. Bazzard.

WITNESS: Thank you, I am going back to the City.

MR. CHESTERTON: I have no intention of cross-examining this witness. That concludes my case.

[SPEECH FOR THE DEFENCE.]

Mr. Chesterton proceeded to address the Court for the defence. He said:

MY LORD, GENTLEMEN OF THE JURY:

I rise to speak in defence of the prisoner in circumstances in many ways difficult and even unfortunate. This is a case which has unfortunately been very much discussed, and very much written about, on which many people have preconceived opinions. I had, indeed, almost thought of appealing to your Lordship to commit at least one well-known man of letters for Contempt of Court, for a very improper article which appeared in yesterday's *Daily Mail*. But, as I say, this is a case which we cannot pretend that any of us comes fresh to. Probably you, Gentlemen of the Jury, have some of you read about it, but I want to point out to you that, situated as you are to-day, you are bound by your oath to give us your decision quite irrespective of any previous opinions which you may have held, quite irrespective of anything that you may have read, or written, or heard; that you are bound to give your opinions on the evidence, on the evidence which has been offered to the Court to-day. And on that evidence I, without a moment's hesitation, claim an acquittal.

What is the situation? Now, apart from the formal witnesses, whose evidence is not much disputed on either side, but to whose evidence I shall have to refer in some detail in a moment—apart from this, we have had two principal witnesses in the box to-day. Now it is obvious that one or other of them is not telling the truth. That is clear and unmistakeable. One of the questions you have to put yourselves is, Which of them was telling the truth, and which was telling falsehoods? You can test that in a good many ways, but whichever way, you will come to the same conclusion—that if there was a witness who was telling the truth it was Thomas Bazzard—if there was a witness who was romancing, it was Miss Helena Landless. What do we know about these two? Mr. Thomas Bazzard is a clerk in the office of a well-known business man; Miss Helena Landless is a young lady from Ceylon. Very much, no doubt, comes from there, but we have learned this evening, as one of the most amazing bits of her evidence, that the old English tavern scores come from there!

Now, let us consider first of all. What about the motives? Here is Bazzard. Bazzard has no motive—no motive whatever—for attempting to secure the release of the prisoner. Miss Helena Landless has admitted in that box on her oath that her hatred of Jasper had nothing whatever to do with the assassination of Edwin Drood. Her hatred of Jasper does not rest on the fact that Jasper has killed Edwin Drood at all. It rests on the fact that Jasper has treated in an unfortunate way her brother, and her friend, Miss Rosa Bud. So there you have her confession that she had a very real motive for hunting down the prisoner. Miss Helena Landless has told her story. She says she was Datchery. What is the first thing that strikes us about that extraordinary story? I asked her whether she made up her face, and she said she did not. Now, had she said that she made up her face, had she said she had painted herself wrinkles, it might have been just possible to ask a sane man to believe that she could go about Cloisterham, where she was well known, and not be recognised: but how can she have the effrontery to go into that box and ask the Jury to believe that she went about the town where she had been living for nine months, and where she was perfectly well known—round the Nuns' House where she had been at school; round Canon Crisparkle's house where she had been a visitor; and round the Cathedral—and that, with her face absolutely unchanged, and merely a white wig and a blue coat! And she asks you to believe that she did that, and that she called on the people who knew her best, and that they did not recognise her! Really, after that, can we be expected to believe one word of her evidence? Really, that is so strong and so monstrous an attempt on our credulity, that I am willing to waive all the other nonsensical parts of her story. There is her way of avoiding suspicion. She wishes to pass as an old buffer. Her idea is to order with a gargantuan meal an enormous quantity of wine and not to drink it! When I pressed her, she said she poured it away. Is it reasonable? It is not necessary to the character of an old buffer that she should drink a pint of sherry. But her whole story! I asked her where she learned to keep tavern scores. Gentlemen, you know what the way of keeping tavern scores means. It is the notorious old English custom of "scoring a man up." As many of you may know, and as Mr. Bazzard has sworn, in evidence, it is a custom particularly of Norfolk. That is a perfectly natural action for Bazzard. Had Miss Landless said a Norfolk man or a countryman had told her, we might have believed her. But she said she learned it in Ceylon! I am rather surprised she did not say it was an accomplishment taught at Miss Twinkleton's! Her theory that she could act as an old buffer is so absurd——because when she was thirteen years old she put on her brother's knickerbockers. It is absurd. As if that would help a woman of 21 to pass as an old buffer! So I unhesitatingly ask you to accept the evidence of Bazzard, and reject that of Miss Helena Landless.

Another important aspect of the matter. If you believe the testimony of Bazzard, which is unshaken—it has not been shaken on one point by my learned friend, and not challenged in one single point—if you believe the evidence of Bazzard, you must acquit the prisoner. You must find the prisoner Not Guilty, because Bazzard has sworn that he has seen the alleged murdered man since the attempted murder. If you believe that, you must acquit the prisoner. But it does not follow—and this point I want particularly to emphasise—it does not follow that if you believe the story of Miss Helena Landless you ought to convict the prisoner. As a matter of fact, Miss Helena Landless has not produced, if her story is true, one little rag of evidence in favour of the guilt of John Jasper. She has, indeed, produced a certain amount of evidence suggesting that he planned an attempt on Edwin Drood's life, but the defence admit that. She has produced a certain amount of evidence that John Jasper thought he had murdered him; but she has produced no rag of evidence that the murder took place. I ask you to believe the evidence of

Bazzard, and I point out that my learned friend has not challenged the evidence of Bazzard.

I took Miss Landless through the whole of her story. She was a wonderfully good witness, but at every point she had to give some extravagant explanation to cover herself. My learned friend, able Counsel as he is, did not ask Bazzard one question hardly about his story. He devoted the whole of his cross-examination to trying to suggest that Bazzard was a great fool, that he had written a bad tragedy which is not in evidence, and that it has not been produced. Suppose he had produced a bad tragedy, and was vain of it. My learned friend may have heard of Frederick the Great, who was very vain of very bad verses. My learned friend has confined himself to saying that he must be telling lies because he is a fool. That is self-contradictory. We have seen him in the box subjected to cross-examination by one of the ablest Counsel at the Bar, and I ask you who saw him to say whether he is a liar or a fool. If he be lying it is impossible to believe that he is not a man of very remarkable ability. The fact that he is a man of low ability is my friend's only reason for calling him a liar! I ask you to believe the testimony of Bazzard; and you must then acquit the prisoner.

But, as I was saying just now, Miss Helena Landless does not produce any evidence; nor does Durdles; nor Canon Crisparkle; not a shred of evidence to show that the murder took place. I had Miss Landless—an able, determined witness—and I challenged her, could she produce one tittle of evidence, other than the ring, to prove that Drood was murdered? and she had to admit, unwillingly, that she could produce none. She said she still retained her opinions. I am sure she would! We can perfectly estimate the attitude of mind of Miss Landless as one of bitter hatred of the prisoner and readiness to believe anything against him. I have no doubt that if Edwin Drood walked into court, she would still think Jasper murdered him. The only thing she can produce is the ring. If you believe Bazzard's evidence, there is no mystery about the ring. It was put there by him. But suppose you don't believe it: there are a hundred ways by which it might have got there. I could give you half a dozen straight away. Jasper might, in going through Edwin's pockets to take out the watch and chain, have dropped the ring in the trance. Drood himself might have taken out the ring and dropped it. There are a hundred possible explanations of the presence of the ring, but there is no possible explanation of the absence of everything else except the ring. Quicklime will destroy the body, but I do ask whether it is conceivable that Edwin Drood had absolutely no metallic objects about him of any kind. I suggest that he might have had metal trouser buttons—unless he was a member of some extraordinary religious community, or some hygienic body which disapproves of anybody wearing anything of the kind!

My friend has made a great deal of the question of the enormous risks. Miss Landless flouted her enormous risks, and Mr. Walters flouted the enormous risks in Bazzard's face. Mr. Bazzard, who is supposed to be a boaster, did not see that he had run such risks. Nor do I. One of the propositions of the prosecution is that Jasper was an extraordinarily brilliant criminal. Of course, he was the reverse. What is admitted by the prosecution itself is ample for my purpose. We say that Jasper bungled the whole thing and did not kill his man; but supposing he did kill him, there is no doubt he bungled. Just think. This clever criminal, who kills a man, is content with his own memory that that man had nothing on him but a watch and chain and pin; drags them out; never thinks he might have some money, although he is staking his neck, or chance of survival, entirely on the assumption that everything will be destroyed by quicklime. He never takes the ordinary precaution to see if there is anything else. It is so amazingly absurd that it would be incredible if we did not know, as we do know, that he was under the influence of a drug and was not master of his faculties when the crime was being committed.

I conclude by just saying this: I am aware that I appear in one sense at a great disadvantage because I am unable to claim any sympathy for my client. I cannot put it to you that my client has been wronged morally by the accusation. I cannot claim your sympathies for him. Undoubtedly he hated his nephew, and planned his murder; undoubtedly he is morally guilty of this murder; but, Gentlemen of the Jury, those things are not within your province. You are not here to judge the soul of John Jasper. You are here to decide whether he has committed the legal crime of murder. Unless that is proved, and proved up to the hilt, you have no right to find him guilty. And I would just say this: if you go beyond your rightful province of pronouncing on that simple matter of fact, you are perhaps thwarting some purpose higher than we know of.

It may not be for nothing that this man has been reserved for this very strange destiny, to have the moral guilt of murder on his head, to have all the remorse for murder in his heart, and yet by a strangely marvellous fate to keep his hand actually free from human blood. Perhaps He who created John Jasper intended for him a destiny more terrible than human punishment, some expiation more terrible than the gallows; and I ask you to give the benefit of the doubt to the prisoner in the dock. Respect upon his brow the sign of that mysterious immunity. Let Cain pass by, for he belongs to God.

[REPLY FOR THE PROSECUTION.]

Mr. Walters then replied for the Prosecution in the following terms:

May it please you, MY LORD, GENTLEMEN OF THE JURY—

Although this case has many complications, the issue itself is an extremely simple one. Was Edwin Drood killed? If so, was Jasper the murderer? The defence has made one amazing, and I think fatal admission. It admits that John Jasper attacked Drood, attacked him with the intention of murdering him, and by that admission it consents that John Jasper's character has gone—that he is a monster, that he is a hypocrite, that he is a man of no moral pretension, that he is a scheming criminal, and that murder was actually in his heart. A stranger defence could scarcely be conceived, and yet there is something in it, because it tries to ride off upon a side issue, and says that "Whereas you may convict this man of a certain attempt, we say that half way there he failed." It is our duty, therefore, to try to prove to you that this man must inevitably have succeeded, and that he knew he had succeeded, and acted as if he had. What are the facts that demonstrated to you most conclusively that John Jasper committed the murder, and that Edwin Drood could not escape? Our contention is that he was the victim of a most carefully and elaborately prepared plot, carried out systematically, arranged most carefully, of such a character that there was no loophole by which he could possibly escape. John Jasper interviewed the right people, chose the exact spot, arranged the very hour when he would have all his material together for the completing of that dreadful task to which he had given himself. He had decided that his rival must be removed—that secret rival who was between him and the great passion, the all-absorbing passion of his life; having once made up his mind, he was inexorable. He knew nothing whatever of pity; he was a complete criminal; and all his acts show that his crime was carried out with a sort of hideous triumph.

But you are asked to believe that he failed, after making all these arrangements, and failed because he was dazed by opium, and only dreamed of the particular act which he thought he had committed. First remember the nature of the attack—the double nature of the attack. It included strangling with a silk scarf, and that was to be followed by the use of quicklime. If Drood escaped the one, surely it was nothing short of a miracle that he escaped the other? And, in any case, if he escaped why should he obligingly disappear to the convenience of the man who attacked him, and to the very great inconvenience of all the friends who loved him? John Jasper was a lasting danger to all who remained behind. Edwin Drood could not so entirely disappear from the realms of civilisation that he would not possibly know what was going on in Cloisterham, and yet you are asked to believe, Gentlemen, that this man upon whom a murderous attack had been made, went away at a convenient moment, leaving his friends to the persecution of the man who had assailed him, and leaving the way clear for the assailant to pursue his own evil courses! I should say it is almost inconceivable—or I should if my learned friend had not so ingeniously conceived it; but that it is believable I don't think you will for a moment agree.

And what definite evidence has been produced to show that Jasper, who had arranged all this for a definite period—Christmas Eve—was suffering from opium at about that time? You have the evidence of Canon Crisparkle that on the very morning of that day, when he met him, he was in wonderfully fine voice, clear-headed, cheerful, in a good temper. All this is absolutely proved by the direct and unimpeached testimony of Canon Crisparkle. Where are the traces of opium? There are no traces of opium. The supreme moment had come, and Jasper was supremely ready for it. There were no traces of opium on him when those two young men departed from his home. He could not have soaked himself in opium during their short absence, and then have recovered in time to make his accusation against Neville Landless by the morning. But you are asked to believe that in that short interval he had time to recover—that he was in a trance so deep that he really thought he had committed a murder which he had not, and yet, early the next morning was so clear-headed, so resolute in purpose, so ready with a connected story which would fix the crime on another person. And why should he have been eager to give the alarm if he had the slightest doubt? A man risen from a trance of opium might have some doubts: but he had none, and within a few hours he was setting things in motion himself, giving the alarm. He had Neville called back, a course he had decided on from the first; he was going to fix the crime on Neville Landless; and within those few hours he had carefully and deliberately carried out the entire scheme. Why this immediate suggestion of murder? Why not a little lapse of time? Because he was confident that the murder had been committed and that the body would not be recovered; and therefore he could be resolute and speedy in his actions, and proceed at once to the second part of the crime which had been the motive for the original crime.

What did he do? Not only did he pursue Neville Landless remorselessly, but he set about persecuting Rosa Bud, whom he could afford to threaten, because he was aware it was safe—that the one rival who had been in his path had been swept out of his way, and that his way was clear. Does a man dazed with opium act in this decisive, rational fashion? He carefully robbed the corpse of those particular jewels of which he had an inventory. My learned friend makes the point—Why did he not feel in his pockets? Why did he not do this, that, and the other? He had inquired of Durdles what quicklime would do. He knew that it would not destroy metal. He had told a jeweller in Cloisterham that he knew exactly what jewellery Edwin had. It consisted of the watch and chain and the scarf pin. It was exactly those things which disappeared and were found in the weir by Canon Crisparkle. What a curious coincidence that the very three things he had an inventory of, and no more, should disappear! And why did he not seek further? Coppers and buttons are no means of certain identification; he could afford to ignore them. Moreover, a murderer does not linger about the body of his victim;

besides, he was already convinced that having removed those three items of jewellery, by which Drood could be identified, he was secure, and the quicklime would do the rest; then he hastened back, for he had to get home again in order to be prepared for the morning, to make his charge against Neville Landless.

But there was one article about Edwin Drood's person of which Jasper knew nothing—the ring, which Drood was to return if his betrothal was broken off, but which we say Grewgious never received. That ring would hold the murderer, and bring him to his doom. It would not be destroyed by the quicklime, and would be there intact and the means of bringing him to the scene of his desperate crime. Remember, he courted inquiry immediately after Drood's disappearance—a sign of his supreme confidence and his colossal audacity. The man who has the slightest doubt that the murder may not have been completed does not at once set the law into motion, go to the magistrate and bring a charge. But if he knows it is completed and the body has gone, he can afford to do so. Everything he had designed to do, he did. It was only something that he did not know of which caused him to bungle. He was not by nature a bungler. He was one of the completest types of criminals that you can imagine, a man who for months and months had been meditating on the closest details of the crime—been to the crypt, talked with Durdles, spoke to Mr. Crisparkle, started his theory that Neville Landless was the person to be charged—and a man who does all those things cannot be accurately described as a bungler.

Canon Crisparkle told you the part Jasper played in fomenting quarrels between Drood and Landless. It is exactly the course that a calculating murderer would pursue. And you have heard the evidence of Durdles, a man who probably scarcely understood the purport of his own remarks. How valuable his testimony was! Jasper had spoken to him of quicklime and of tombs, and Jasper had gone with him on a midnight expedition. Was all this vain and useless? Was the expedition at midnight merely a pleasant little picnic for no particular purpose, or merely for fun? Not for fun, when we find that it all fits the composite scheme of murder which was carried out.

My learned friend has spoken about Helena Landless. I say she is a witness entirely beyond reproach. She was the very woman framed by nature to carry out her arduous part. She had every need for her action and the capacity for her daring work—every essential qualification for that difficult part was possessed in advance by Helena Landless. She had had experience; in her youth she had dressed as a boy, and shown the daring of a man; she was the leader of her brother, and when everything else had failed, when six months had passed by and she was able to do nothing by ordinary means, she adopted this extraordinary means of disguise in order to carry out her work. We are asked why she did not paint her face. I don't know whether my learned friend wanted her to black her face or what he wanted her to do; but she was brought up in a warm climate with a rich dark complexion and she chose the part of the "old buffer," which means, if it means anything, something of the sailor type. Her complexion was ready for her. She wore a large white wig to hide her luxuriant tresses. Why Bazzard should wear a large wig I don't know. She had the only effective disguise for her, the disguise of an elderly man, because she had to live up to the white wig to conceal her woman's figure. She was no stranger in Cloisterham and was perfectly equal to the task of conversing with those whom she had already met before.

One word on Bazzard. If you reject Helena Landless, there is only one alternative. You must put Thomas Bazzard in her place. Is this Mr. Bazzard, the man who fell asleep while his employer was discussing crucial matters with a client, one who was likely to appear as the elderly Mr. Datchery in Cloisterham? This man, who thinks more of his drama than his law work, is he a likely man to have devoted himself to confronting a man already suspected of murder? You have seen a Mr. Bazzard in the box, and I put it to you that he was specially got up to produce a false impression upon you. The Bazzard in the box was bright and alert and voluble. The official record says that he was "a pale, puffy-faced, dark-haired person of thirty, with big dark eyes that wholly wanted lustre, and a dissatisfied, doughy complexion that seemed to ask to be sent to the baker's." That is the gentleman who was to act the part of the brave and daring Datchery! I say it is impossible, and that his own vanity has tempted him to claim these honours. He told you he "placed" the ring in the crypt for any passer-by to pick up, and that, knowing Drood was alive, he still allowed Neville Landless to be accused of murder and Rosa Bud to be persecuted by Jasper. This from a man connected with law! It is an absurd story, and utterly incredible. I ask you to reject it.

Gentlemen, a solemn duty rests on you in this crisis which I am sure gentlemen of your ability and intelligence will faithfully discharge. It is with infinite pain that I have to ask that this man shall pay the penalty of his sin. But John Jasper himself showed no mercy. He fondled the victim whom he intended to butcher; he lured to his doom one who he had made to feel was his nearest and dearest friend; he destroyed a life full of promise, a life which might have been fruitful and happy. I do not ask for vengeance, but only for the fulfilment of the law, that justice may be trusted to maintain the sanctity of human life. If you fail in your duty this man will henceforth be free. I charge you, in the name of humanity and human rights, to quit you as men, to act on the facts which have been placed before you. This mystery, Gentlemen, has lasted long enough. It is in your power to-day to elucidate what has seemed to be obscure, to solve this deep and complex problem.

Yours is an enviable opportunity, and to-day you may strike a very great blow for the truth. The eyes of the nation are upon you, the whole world is anxiously awaiting your decision. I beg you, Gentlemen, resolutely and earnestly to sweep away all this fantasy which has been placed before you by my learned friend, to forget his extraordinary story of a half murder, which I think I have shown to be impossible, and by one bold and emphatic stroke to solve for ever the Mystery of Edwin Drood.

[THE SUMMING UP.]

His Lordship then proceeded to sum up, as follows:

GENTLEMEN OF THE JURY—

You will not be the first Jury empanelled in this great country who will have to come to your decision with unreasonable speed. The proceedings have been so interesting that I cannot hope to do them justice; but I will merely go over, as far as I can, the main features of the case, and then my duty will be to leave it to you. First of all, it should be remembered, because it is indeed included in what is referred to as the Official Record——

A SPECTATOR: Louder, please.

JUDGE: I am speaking to the Jury. If you think you can hang that man for us, you are mistaken.—I say it is included even in the Official Record by an indirect admission that we owe a great deal of information that we have heard this evening to a man of letters. I must therefore ask the Gentlemen of the Jury to put themselves for one moment in the position of such a person. You must forget that you are solid and good citizens summoned to decide a serious matter, nay, I must forget that I am an experienced Judge seated on this Bench for many years; and we must all try to think—both the Jury and myself—try to think we are authors. Supposing that to be the case, it is all the easier, of course, to imagine oneself the author of a crime. I will, therefore, very rapidly divide up the evidence, as I see it, on the two sides, and then leave the matter to you.

I need not tell you how serious is the issue put before you. If it were only the solemnity of ending the Mystery of Edwin Drood it would be almost as solemn as that of ending a human life, but if any doubt exists in your minds at all as to whether the Mystery of Edwin Drood has been solved by the prosecution, you must permit the prisoner in the dock to go forth, even if from a merely personal study of his countenance you think he is going forth to murder other people. Unless the prosecution has convinced you that the Mystery is at an end, you have no right to convict him, and he has the right to the benefit of the doubt.

The next thing necessary clearly to distinguish is the evidence of the two principal witnesses. The others were rather entertainers than witnesses. There were two very genuine witnesses, one of whom perjured himself or herself—that is to say, would have done so had we permitted profanity to enter into these proceedings. I want to say one thing about that. It is a remarkable fact, and in that point the Jury ought to really fairly balance their minds, because there is a case for possible perjury in both instances. So horrible a crime as perjury can only be committed either from a very low or a very high motive. The character of Mr. Bazzard, as revealed by himself with picturesque clearness, appears to me an entertaining and attractive but, shall I say? not a saintly character, and it appears to me to be arguable that he might possibly tell a lie from general amusement at the absurd way in which the world is run. On the other hand, it is admitted, I think, for Miss Landless that though she would not tell a lie or forswear herself for money, she might conceivably do it as counting religious observance beneath some affection she had for her brother. I therefore put it to the Jury as possible that both are liars. But I should distinguish between their motives if I were writing a spiritual treatise. It is tenable in both cases. Undoubtedly if one is telling the truth the other is lying.

About the wearing of a wig, I think the point has been somewhat unduly pressed on one side. I think it is a strong argument for Datchery being Helena Landless, but not a very strong one that she feels the weight of the wig. I suppose there are many of us here this evening who have been not unconscious of the discomfort of wearing a wig when you have too much hair already. So I should not press forward the argument that it must have been a woman's hair—or I should not press it too far. Edwin Drood is represented in the picture as having monstrously long hair—but that does not concern us here. I think it should be conceded as a point, but not a very great point, to the prosecution. We come to the second broad distinction which amounts to this: that very few of the witnesses, and I daresay very few of the Jurymen, are acquainted with the proper use and enjoyment of two substances, one of which is opium, and the other quicklime. Most of us, I conceive, indulge in these things, if at all, in great moderation, but anyhow, a great deal depends upon the operation of these two things; and it appears to me on that point that the whole of this Court, not having called any expert evidence, either of morphia maniacs, or of persons partially buried in quicklime, (who are, I imagine a select class)—as the trial has not called any kind of technical evidence about the effects of these things, I think it my duty to put it to the Jury that they must reserve their judgment and allow a wide space for human ignorance about the effects of these things. I certainly do not know how quick opium confuses the mind, or how quick quicklime destroys the body, and if the Jury know it, I, in the best traditions of the Bench and Bar, command that they dismiss it from their minds.

We have placed in front of us two allegations. On the one side it is alleged by the prosecution that there is, after all is said and done, a very strong argument for the death of Drood, in the fact that he did not return; it is alleged by the defence that you have an even stronger argument against any theory of the murder of Edwin Drood, because, again, he did not return, even as a corpse. "If he is dead," says the defence, "where is the corpse?" "If he is alive," says the prosecution, "where is he?" That, I think, is a fair summary of the arguments, and it is obvious that if you come to think it out, these two theories depend on those two suppositions. Is it possible for opium to make a person half commit a murder? or Is it possible for quicklime so to destroy all traces, including buttons, and so that the disappearance of the body is evidence of the murder? That is the question I shall leave entirely to you—as to whether there is enough of what I may truly call "quicklime evidence" to warrant you regarding Jasper as a real murderer, or enough of "opium evidence" to warrant you saying that it was a visionary or dream murder. Those, I should say, would be the broad lines on which you have to decide. For the rest, you have to be answerable to the highest conceivable Authority as to how you deal with a very fascinating romance. Gentlemen of the Jury, you will retire and consider your verdict.

[THE VERDICT.]

Immediately his Lordship had concluded, the Foreman of the Jury rose and said:

MY LORD,—I am happy to be able to announce to your Lordship that we, following the tradition and practice of British Juries, have arranged our verdict in the luncheon interval. I should explain, my Lord, that it undoubtedly presented itself to us as a point of extraordinary difficulty in this case, that a man should disappear absolutely and completely, having cut off all communication with his friends in Cloisterham; but having seen and heard the society and conversation of Cloisterham here in Court to-day, we no longer feel the slightest surprise at that. Now, under the influence of that observation, my Lord, the more extreme characters, if they will allow me to say so, in this Jury, were at first inclined to find a verdict of Not Guilty, because there was no evidence of a murder having been committed; but on the other hand, the calmer and more judicious spirits among us felt that to allow a man who had committed a cold-blooded murder of which his own nephew was the victim, to leave the dock absolutely unpunished, was a proceeding which would probably lead to our all being murdered in our beds. And so you will be glad to learn that the spirit of compromise and moderation prevailed, and we find the prisoner guilty of Manslaughter.

We recommend him most earnestly to your Lordship's mercy, whilst at the same time begging your Lordship to remember that the protection of the lives of the community is in your hands, and begging you not to allow any sentimental consideration to deter you from applying the law in its utmost vigour.

MR. WALTERS: I should like to urge that the Jury be discharged for not having performed their duties in the proper spirit of the law. We have heard from the Foreman that the verdict was arranged in advance, and I decline to accept that verdict, and ask for your Lordship's ruling.

THE FOREMAN: The Jury, like all British Juries, will be only too delighted to be discharged at the earliest moment: the sooner the better.

MR. CHESTERTON: I want to associate myself with my learned friend.

JUDGE: My decision is that everybody here, except myself, be committed for Contempt of Court. Off you all go to prison without any trial whatever!

The Court rose at 11.35, the actual hearing having occupied four hours and twenty minutes.

FOOTNOTES:

[2] Each Juryman had been supplied with a copy of the book in the 1*s.* edition.

Milton Keynes UK
Ingram Content Group UK Ltd.
UKHW030742071024
449371UK00006B/622